Betty Crocker's

BEST BARBECUE RECIPES

Betty Crocker's

BEST BARBECUE RECIPES

PRENTICE HALL

New York London Toronto Sydney Tokyo Singapore

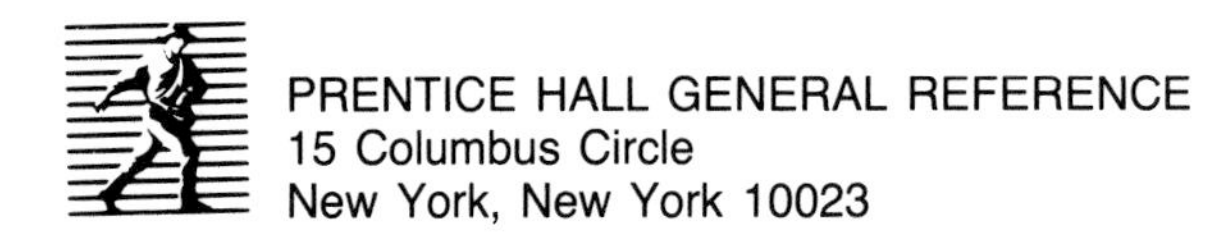
PRENTICE HALL GENERAL REFERENCE
15 Columbus Circle
New York, New York 10023

Library of Congress Cataloging-in-Publication Data

Crocker, Betty.
[Best barbecue recipes]
Betty Crocker's best barbecue recipes.
p. cm.
Includes index.
ISBN: 0-671-86517-X
1. Barbecue cookery. I. Title. II. Title: Best barbecue recipes.
TX840.B3C79 1993
641.5'784—dc20 92-34873
CIP

Designed by Levavi & Levavi, Inc.
Manufactured in the United States of America

10 9 8 7 6 5 4 3 2 1

First Edition

Front cover: Grilled Shrimp and Scallop Kabobs (page 55)
Back cover: Hamburgers Supreme (page 9)

Contents

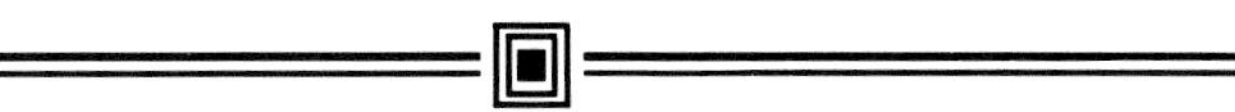

Introduction

Just about everyone loves to barbecue, whether it's on a backyard grill, at a picnic site, on a balcony hibachi, a stovetop grill—or in a pinch—under the oven broiler. Food cooked with an open flame just always seems to taste better!

We have all become more adventuresome in what we cook on the barbecue, branching out into vegetables, fish, chicken, breads and even desserts. *Betty Crocker's Best Barbecue Recipes* offers recipes for the wide range of foods that can be successfully cooked on your barbecue. Of course, you'll find the great barbecue classics gathered here: many varieties of juicy hamburgers, wonderfully flavored steaks, fun and easy franks, and delicious ribs.

But we have also collected recipes to inspire you and give you ideas for new ways to enjoy your grill. Moreover, you'll find complete directions for grilling fish and chicken, along with enticing recipes such as Monteray Fish Steaks, Grilled Texas Shrimp, whole Stuffed Fish, Chicken Afganistan, Apple-stuffed Chicken Breasts and whole Herb-Smoked Chicken. And with our section on sauces and marinades, you can take everyday chicken, meat, fish or vegetables and make them special.

There's also a section on grilling vegetables, from satisfying corn on the cob to sophisticated Grilled Eggplant Dip. You'll also find breads to round out your meal, such as Hickory Cheese Bread. We included dessert too! Try Pound Cake S'mores or Zucchini Nut Cakes for a change-of-pace ending to your favorite grilled dinner.

With complete information on the various types of grills as well as grilling safety and tips throughout on turning out great barbecued meals, *Betty Crocker's Best Barbecue Recipes* is a welcome addition to the library of both beginning and experienced barbecue cooks.

THE BETTY CROCKER EDITORS

Barbecue Basics

Barbecuing is a simple pleasure, but you do need to do a little barbecue homework, then take a few trial runs to build confidence. The following information will help you grill expertly and easily.

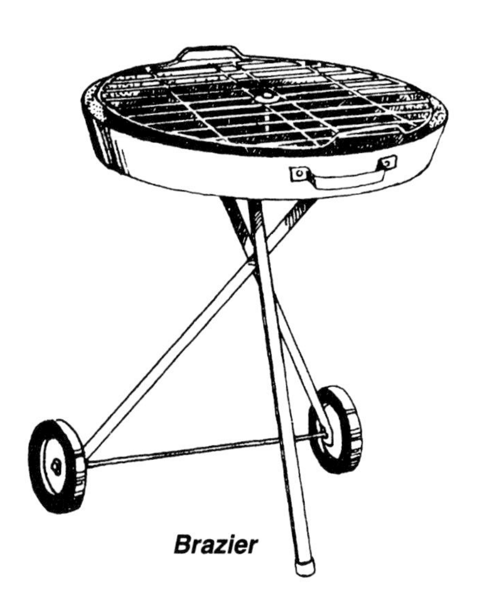

Brazier

THE GRILLWORKS

The first thing to think about is what kind of outdoor grill is best for your needs. The following will give you a good idea of the grills available. Add to this your own outdoor cooking preferences and pick the grill that's best for you.

Braziers: In its simplest form, a brazier consists of a shallow firebox to hold the charcoal and a metal cooking grill for the food. It may have 3 or 4 legs, long or short, foldable or stationary. A lazy Susan cooking grill and/or supports at different levels can be used to help control heat and are integral parts of most models. Some braziers also have accessories that make more complicated cooking procedures possible.

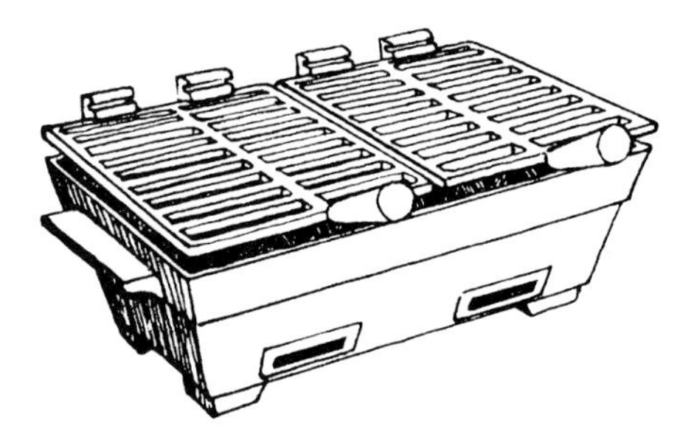

Hibachi

Hibachis: Of Japanese origin, these grills are very portable, permitting you to do on-the-spot cooking almost anywhere. They are heavy for their size, but this metal weight provides a heat-holding quality that's ideal for outdoor cooking. The single hibachi is perfect for cooking small amounts of food; double and triple models are also available.

Covered kettle cookers: Made of heavy cast metal and available in a variety of sizes, these are more sophisticated members of the brazier family. They have air-flow vents, both top and bottom, that help control the heat. They are relatively expensive, but with the multitude of available accessories—motorized rotisseries, skewers with racks, rib racks and roast holders—they offer an almost limitless world of outdoor cooking.

Covered Kettle

Gas and electric grills: The shapes and designs of these grills are derived from those of their charcoal cousins, but here charcoal cooking takes a back seat to the modern age. Gas is used to heat semi-permanent lava briquets that act as the cooking "coals." If you are concerned that the charcoal flavor will be missing, don't worry. Actually, it is the smoke created when the drippings hit the hot coals (be they charcoal or lava) that accounts for most of the flavor. Gas grills are available as portables (fed by small propane tanks) or as stationaries (connected to your regular gas supply). Electric grills are fast, but they are somewhat limited in mobility because they must be connected to safely grounded outlets or extensions. Always follow the manufacturer's directions carefully when using gas or electric grills.

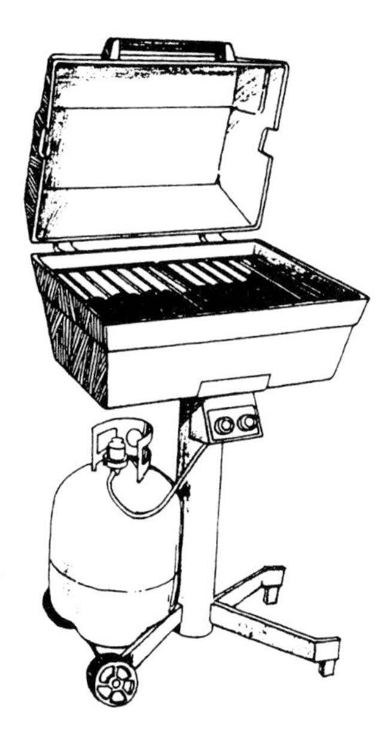

Gas Grill

Smokers: These "slow-cookers" are available in either charcoal or electric models. Ranging from simple to quite complicated units, they promise—and deliver—food with a unique smoky flavor.

Smoker

GRILLING WITH CHARCOAL

One important point to remember about grilling with charcoal: Damp charcoal can put a damper on the whole meal by taking forever to start. So take heed and store your charcoal in a dry place.

How Much to Use?

Don't overdo. Charcoal is a real heat producer and a little goes a long way. For 4 to 6 servings of a quick-cooking food (hamburgers, for example), use 20 to 30 briquets; 40 to 50 are about right for longer-cooking foods (roasts, pork, poultry, whole fish). You'll need enough briquets to form a solid bed of coals under the grilling area. Any meat or poultry that grills longer than one hour will require about 10 additional briquets per hour. Always follow the manufacturer's directions concerning the amount of additional briquets recommended for your particular grill. Be sure to place added briquets around the edges so they touch the already-burning coals.

Getting the Fire Going

Place the desired number of briquets in the firebox and arrange them in a slight pyramid shape to get them ready for lighting. (The pyramid shape allows air to circulate, heating the briquets faster.)

If using an electric starter, pyramid the briquets over the coil and plug in. After the briquets have been started (8 to 12 minutes), unplug and remove the starter to an out-of-the-way, fireproof spot. The coals will be ready for grilling in another 15 to 20 minutes.

If using a liquid starter, follow the manufacturer's directions. (Use only liquid starters especially intended for charcoal—never use gasoline or kerosene.) Drizzle the starter liberally over the pyramid and wait about a minute, then ignite the outer edges of the briquets with a match. Stand back in case of flareups. The coals will be ready for grilling in 25 to 45 minutes. Once the fire is under way, never use liquid starter to "speed things up"—the danger of flare-ups and the possibility of an uncontrollable fire is far too great.

No matter how you start the fire, the coals will be ready for grilling when they have a light, even coating of gray ash. Red coals are too hot; black coals too cool; a mix of red and black coals gives off uneven heat.

Controlling the Heat

As soon as the coals are ready for grilling, spread them in a single layer in an even pattern just slightly larger than the area covered by the food on the cooking grill. You can check the temperature by placing your hand, palm-side-down, near but not touching the cooking grill. If you have to pull your hand away in less than 2 seconds, the coals are too hot; wait 5 to 10 minutes or until your hand can take the heat for 4 to 5 seconds. That means the coals are medium—a good temperature for cooking.

Try to keep the heat as even as possible throughout the grilling period. If you're not getting a sizzle, the fire may be too cool. To raise the heat, rake the coals closer together and knock off a bit of the ash, lower the cooking grill or open the vents. For a too-hot fire, do just the opposite—spread and separate the coals, raise the cooking grill or partially close the vents. Choose the method most appropriate for your grill. Remember, too, the cooking time will be faster on hot, calm days and slower on chilly, windy ones.

Occasional flare-ups are part and parcel of grilling. Although they can be controlled easily by spacing out the coals or covering the grill, a spray of water can be just as effective. Just don't get carried away and soak the coals.

COOKING WITH GAS AND ELECTRICITY

Both gas and electric grills are instant starters, heat up quickly, are easy to control and can continue to supply the desired cooking temperature as long as you want.

Special features you may want to look for in gas grills include porcelain-coated cooking grills (helps to resist corrosion and makes clean-up easier), a handle designed to be gripped easily and comfortably (not too close to the firebox), a fuel gauge so you won't be caught short and an easily replaceable fuel tank.

Starting the Gas Grill

Preheat the grill according to the manufacturer's directions. If the weather is cool or windy, a slightly longer warm-up time as well as a higher setting will speed along the cooking.

Controlling the Heat

You can regulate the heat by adjusting the control, repositioning the cooking grill or covering the grill. The heat varies from brand to brand. A gas grill also has faster and slower cooking areas. Once you map these out, however, you can use them to produce different degrees of doneness. If your gas grill has dual control burners, you can cook by indirect heat. Light only one side of the grill and cook the food on the opposite side. To brown the meat, move it directly over the flame.

Grill Care

Unlike charcoal briquets, the lava briquets in a gas grill can be used over and over. But you can avoid flare-ups and lengthen the life of the briquets by turning them over every once in a while, between cooking times, to burn off the grease that accumulates from cooking meat. To avoid corrosion on metal parts of the grill, remove foods from the grill before salting.

GRILLING UTENSILS

These utensils and supplies make grilling a breeze:

- A hinged wire grill basket is especially helpful for grilling delicate foods and small pieces of foods. If you don't have a grill basket, try improvising with two metal cooling racks wired together.
- Long-handled utensils, such as tongs, forks, spatulas and basting brushes keep the heat at a safe distance.
- Keep a spray bottle full of cool water nearby to put out flare-ups. Light spritzes of water are usually adequate.
- Use fire-resistant mitts and pot holders to protect your hands.
- Aluminum foil pans are handy for heating sauces right on the grill.
- A stiff wire brush helps make cleaning the cooking surface easier.

GRILLING SAFETY

To grill safely, follow these simple tips:

- Place the grill on level ground where it will stand steady.
- Never use gasoline or kerosene in place of liquid starter made especially for charcoal grilling.
- Never add liquid starter to briquets that have already been lit. The danger of the fire flaring up is great.
- Gas tanks must be handled with care. It is important to secure the tank when moving the grill. When the tank is connected to the regulator, do not let it tip.
- When attaching a gas tank to the grill, check the connection with liquid detergent. The appearance of bubbles indicates a leak.
- Store gas tanks and liquid starters away from the house.
- Grill only in well-ventilated areas, never in an enclosed space.
- Woods that are not suitable for smoking include pine, cedar, spruce and eucalyptus. Their smoke is acrid.
- Do not leave a fire unattended. Children should have supervision around grills.

HOW TO TELL WHEN FOOD IS DONE

Follow recipe guidelines for cooking times and for internal temperatures, where applicable.

When using a meat thermometer, insert it so that the tip rests in the center of the thickest part of the meat, but does not touch bone or rest in

TABLE OF INTERNAL TEMPERATURES

Beef and Lamb	
rare	140°F
medium	160°F
well	175°F
Fish, fresh (not frozen)	175°F
Pork	
fresh cuts	170°F
smoked cuts:	
arm picnic (cook before eating)	170°F
loin or ham (cook before eating)	160°F
fully cooked ham, Canadian-style bacon or arm picnic	140°F
Turkey	185°F

fat. (See chart above for internal temperatures.) In the case of turkey, place the tip in the thickest part of the thigh. For additional indications of doneness after the minimum cooking time, press the meat lightly with protected fingers. If the juices run red, the food is not sufficiently cooked. If they run pink in the case of beef or lamb, that is fine for those who enjoy their meat rare. However, for pork or poultry, a few minutes more cooking time is necessary if the juices run pink.

Chicken is done when the juices run clear, the leg meat feels very soft between protected fingers and the leg of a whole bird moves easily. (These signs also apply to turkey, goose, duck, capon, Cornish game hens and quail.) Fish is done when the meat flakes easily with a fork. To test, insert a fork at an angle into the thickest part of the fish and twist gently.

HOW TO USE NUTRITION INFORMATION

Nutrition Information Per Serving for each recipe includes the amounts of calories, protein, carbohydrate, fat, cholesterol and sodium.

- If ingredient choices are given, the first listed ingredient is used in recipe nutrition information calculations.
- When ingredient ranges or more than one serving size is indicated, the first weight or serving is used to calculate nutrition information.
- "If desired" ingredients and recipe variations are not included in nutrition information calculations.

Menus

EASY FAMILY DINNER
Hamburgers Supreme (page 9)
Spicy Grilled Corn (page 64)
Potatoes in Foil (page 66)
Sliced Tomatoes
Pound Cake S'mores (page 72)
Milk

RAINY DAY BARBECUE
Italian Sausage Kabobs (use Broiler variation) (page 21)
Tossed Green Salad
Bruschetta on the Grill (page 71)
Ice Cream Sundaes
Iced Tea

SOUTHWEST SIZZLE
Grilled Chicken Adobo (page 29)
Sliced Avocados and Red Onions
Grilled Lime Tortillas (page 71)
Golden Pears (page 75)
Lemonade or Sangria

BARBECUE FOR A CROWD
Herbed Butterflied Leg of Lamb (page 15)
Grilled Vegetables
Bread in Foil with Garlic Butter Spread (page 72)
Grilled Shortcake (page 75)
Fruit Punch

CATCH OF THE DAY
Lime Fish Fillets (page 43)
Grilled Zucchini with Basil (page 64)
Grilled Onions (page 65)
Zesty Grilled Potatoes (page 67)
Pineapple-Angel Food Dessert (page 72)
Wine Spritzers or Flavored Seltzer

BARBECUE FOR LUNCH
Grilled Chicken Sandwiches (page 37)
Coleslaw
Cut-up Vegetables
Watermelon and Cookies
Fruit Juice

Grilled Steak with Sesame Butter

1

Meat on the Grill

Grilled Steak with Flavored Butters

Steaks are great on the grill, and with this timetable, they'll always be cooked just the way you like them!

1/3- to 3/4-pound steak with bone or 1/3- to 1/2-pound boneless steak per serving
Salt and pepper to taste
Flavored Butters (right)

Choose beef tenderloin (filet mignon), T-bone, porterhouse, sirloin, rib or rib eye steak. Slash outer edge of fat on steak diagonally at 1-inch intervals to prevent curling (do not cut into lean).

Grill steak 4 to 5 inches from medium coals, turning once, until desired doneness (see Timetable). Sprinkle with salt and pepper after turning. Remove from grill; top with flavored butter. **4 servings**

PER SERVING: Calories 200; Protein 37 g; Carbohydrate 0 g; Fat 6 g; Cholesterol 100 mg; Sodium 70 mg

TO BROIL: Set oven control to broil. Place steak on rack in broiler pan; place broiler pan so top of 3/4- to 1-inch steak is 2 to 3 inches from heat, 1- to 2-inch steak is 3 to 5 inches from heat. Broil, turning once, until desired doneness (see timetable).

Sprinkle with salt and pepper after turning and after removing from broiler; top with flavored butter.

Mustard Butter

1/4 cup (1/2 stick) margarine or butter, softened
1 tablespoon chopped fresh parsley
2 tablespoons prepared mustard
1/4 teaspoon onion salt

Beat all ingredients.

Sesame Butter

1/4 cup (1/2 stick) margarine or butter, softened
1 teaspoon Worcestershire sauce
1/2 teaspoon garlic salt
1 tablespoon toasted sesame seed

Beat margarine, Worcestershire sauce and garlic salt. Stir in sesame seed.

TIMETABLE FOR BROILING OR GRILLING BEEF STEAK

CUT	APPROXIMATE TOTAL COOKING TIME*
Tenderloin (filet mignon, 4 to 8 ounces)	15 to 20 minutes
T-bone Steak	
1 inch	25 minutes
1 1/2 inches	35 minutes
Porterhouse Steak	
1 inch	25 minutes
1 1/2 inches	35 minutes
Sirloin Steak	
1 inch	25 minutes
1 1/2 inches	35 minutes
Rib or Rib Eye Steak	
1 inch	20 minutes
1 1/2 inches	30 minutes
2 inches	45 minutes

**Time given is for medium doneness (160°).*

Barbecued London Broil

Marinating tenderizes the flank steak.

1/3 cup white vinegar
1/3 cup vegetable oil
3 tablespoons packed brown sugar
3 tablespoons soy sauce
2 medium onions, sliced
1 clove garlic, crushed
1/2 teaspoon coarsely ground pepper
1 1/2-pound beef flank steak

Mix all ingredients except beef flank steak; pour over beef in a glass dish. Cover and refrigerate, turning beef 2 or 3 times, at least 4 hours.

Remove beef and onions; reserve marinade. Cover and grill beef 4 to 5 inches from medium coals, turning and brushing 2 or 3 times with reserved marinade, until desired doneness, 10 to 15 minutes for medium. Cook and stir onions in skillet on grill until warm. Cut beef diagonally across the grain into very thin slices; serve with onions. **6 servings**

PER SERVING: Calories 205; Protein 24 g; Carbohydrate 3 g; Fat 11 g; Cholesterol 65 mg; Sodium 190 mg

Steak Tips

- To prevent the rim of fat around a steak or chop from curling, diagonally slash the outer edge of fat at 1-inch intervals. Be careful not to cut into the lean.
- When testing for doneness, make the cut close to the bone.
- Season each side of the steak only after it has browned nicely. Salt tends to draw moisture to the surface, delaying browning.

Mexican Grilled Steak

2 high-quality beef flank steaks (1 to 1 1/2 pounds each)
Juice of 2 limes (about 1/2 cup)
4 cloves garlic, crushed
1/3 cup chopped fresh or 2 tablespoons dried oregano leaves
2 tablespoons olive or vegetable oil
2 teaspoons salt
1/2 teaspoon pepper

Place beef steaks in shallow glass or plastic dish. Mix remaining ingredients; pour over beef. Cover and refrigerate at least 8 hours but no longer than 24 hours, turning beef occasionally.

Cover and grill beef 4 to 5 inches from medium coals, turning once, until desired doneness, 10 to 15 minutes for medium. Cut beef across grain at slanted angle into thin slices. Serve with tortillas and guacamole if desired. **8 servings**

PER SERVING: Calories 200; Protein 24 g; Carbohydrate 2 g; Fat 12 g; Cholesterol 65 mg; Sodium 600 mg

TO BROIL: Marinate beef steaks as directed above. Set oven control to broil. Place beef on rack in broiler pan. Broil with tops 2 to 3 inches from heat until brown, about 5 minutes. Turn beef; broil 5 minutes longer. Cut and serve as directed above.

Mexican Grilled Steak

Steak with Peppercorns

Using your broiler is a handy option if it rains!

3 tablespoons cracked black peppercorns
6 boneless sirloin steaks (about 3/4 inch thick)
1 tablespoon margarine or butter
1/4 cup finely chopped shallots
1/4 cup brandy or beef broth
1/2 cup beef broth
1/2 cup sour cream

Press peppercorns into both sides of steaks. Grill steaks 5 to 6 inches from medium coals 3 to 5 minutes per side or until desired doneness.

Melt margarine in medium saucepan over medium heat; add shallots. Cook about 2 minutes until shallots are tender. Stir in brandy and broth; cook over medium-high heat about 5 minutes or until mixture is slightly reduced. Stir in sour cream. Serve with steaks. **6 servings**

PER SERVING: Calories 275; Protein 39 g; Carbohydrate 3 g; Fat 12 g; Cholesterol 115 mg; Sodium 160 mg

TO BROIL: Set oven control to broil. Place steaks on rack in broiler pan; place pan 2 to 3 inches from heat. Broil 10 minutes; turn steaks. Broil 8 to 10 minutes or until desired doneness.

Mushroom- and Garlic-stuffed Sirloin

4 ounces finely chopped mushrooms (about 1 cup)
12 cloves garlic, finely chopped (about 1/4 cup)
4 green onions (with tops), sliced
1 tablespoon vegetable oil
2 teaspoons chopped fresh or 1/2 teaspoon dried marjoram leaves
1/4 teaspoon salt
1/4 teaspoon pepper
3-pound beef boneless top sirloin steak, 2 inches thick

Cook mushrooms, garlic and onions in oil in 10-inch skillet, stirring frequently, until garlic is golden brown; remove from heat. Stir in marjoram, salt and pepper; cool.

Make a horizontal cut in side of beef steak, forming a pocket (do not cut through opposite side). Spoon mushroom mixture into pocket, spreading evenly. Secure with toothpicks.

Grill beef 4 to 5 inches from medium coals 1 minute on each side to seal in juices. Cover and grill beef 25 to 30 minutes for medium doneness, turning once. Remove toothpicks. Cut beef into 1/2-inch slices. **9 servings**

PER SERVING: Calories 275; Protein 32 g; Carbohydrate 1 g; Fat 15 g; Cholesterol 95 mg; Sodium 140 mg

Grilled Florentine Steaks

Beginning with an unadorned steak, then adding flavored olive oil gives this steak Italian flair.

1/4 cup chopped fresh parsley
1/4 cup olive oil
1 teaspoon salt
1 teaspoon pepper
4 cloves garlic, cut into pieces
4 beef T-bone steaks, about 1 inch thick

Place all ingredients except beef steaks in food processor or blender. Cover and process until smooth.

Cover and grill beef about 4 inches from hot coals 16 minutes, turning once and brushing with oil mixture frequently, until done.

4 servings

PER SERVING: Calories 370; Protein 34 g; Carbohydrate 2 g; Fat 25 g; Cholesterol 90 mg; Sodium 620 mg

TO BROIL: Set oven control to broil. Slash diagonally outer edge of fat on beef steaks at 1-inch intervals to prevent curling (do not cut into lean). Place beef on rack in broiler pan. Broil with tops 2 to 3 inches from heat 10 minutes, brushing with oil mixture frequently, until brown. Turn beef; broil 10 to 15 minutes, brushing with oil mixture frequently, until beef is done.

Pepper and Onion Roast

An inexpensive roast turned into a very special entrée.

3-pound beef cross rib pot roast, about 1 1/2 inches thick
1 envelope (.8 ounce) meat marinade
2 large bell peppers, cut into 1/4-inch strips
1 large white or red onion, cut into halves and thinly sliced
1/4 cup olive or vegetable oil
1 clove garlic, crushed
1 tablespoon vinegar
1 teaspoon dried oregano leaves
1/2 teaspoon salt
1/4 teaspoon pepper

Marinate beef roast as directed on envelope. Cook and stir bell peppers and onion in oil in 10-inch skillet over medium heat until crisp-tender, 3 to 5 minutes. Stir in remaining ingredients; remove from heat.

Cover and grill beef 4 to 5 inches from medium coals, turning 2 or 3 times, until desired doneness, 40 to 50 minutes for medium. Heat pepper and onion mixture in skillet on grill, stirring occasionally, until warm; serve with beef.

9 servings

PER SERVING: Calories 440; Protein 40 g; Carbohydrate 4 g; Fat 29 g; Cholesterol 120 mg; Sodium 500 mg

Grilled Meat and Vegetable Kabobs

Grilled Meat and Vegetable Kabobs

1-pound lamb boneless shoulder, cut into 1-inch cubes
1 pound veal or beef tenderloin, cut into 1-inch cubes
½ cup Pesto
½ cup dry white wine or chicken broth
3 tablespoons lemon juice
8 ounces fresh medium mushrooms, stems removed
1 red bell pepper, cut into 1-inch pieces
1 green bell pepper, cut into 1-inch pieces
1 yellow bell pepper, cut into 1-inch pieces
16 fresh bay or sage leaves
2 leeks, cut into 1-inch pieces
8 cherry tomatoes

Place lamb and veal in glass or plastic bowl. Mix pesto, wine and lemon juice; pour over meat. Cover and refrigerate 1 hour.

Remove meat from marinade; reserve marinade. Alternate meat, mushrooms, bell pepper pieces, bay leaves and leek pieces on each of eight 9-inch metal skewers, leaving space between each piece of food. Top each skewer with tomato.

Cover and grill kabobs about 4 inches from hot coals 16 minutes, turning once and brushing with marinade occasionally, until meat is done. **4 servings**

PER SERVING: Calories 575; Protein 66 g; Carbohydrate 13 g; Fat 29 g; Cholesterol 230 mg; Sodium 400 mg

TO BROIL: Set oven control to broil. Place kabobs on rack in broiler pan. Broil with tops about 3 inches from heat 5 minutes. Turn kabobs; brush with marinade. Broil 5 minutes. Turn kabobs; brush with marinade. Broil 5 minutes longer or until meat is done.

Beef and Corn Kabobs

An easy meal, all on a skewer!

½ cup vegetable oil
¼ cup red wine vinegar
1 tablespoon chopped fresh or 1 teaspoon dried thyme leaves
½ teaspoon ground red pepper (cayenne)
1 clove garlic, finely chopped
1½-pound beef boneless top round steak, cut into 1-inch cubes
4 small ears corn, husks removed
2 bell peppers, cut into 1½-inch pieces

Mix oil, vinegar, thyme, red pepper and garlic in medium glass or plastic bowl. Add beef; stir to coat with marinade. Cover and refrigerate at least 4 hours, stirring occasionally.

Cut each ear of corn into 3 pieces. Remove beef from marinade; reserve marinade. Thread beef alternately with corn and bell peppers about ¼ inch apart on six 11-inch metal skewers. Brush generously with marinade.

Cover and grill 4 to 5 inches from medium coals 15 to 20 minutes for medium doneness, turning the kabobs frequently and brushing with marinade. **6 servings**

PER SERVING: Calories 285; Protein 31 g; Carbohydrate 16 g; Fat 11 g; Cholesterol 85 mg; Sodium 80 mg

Teriyaki Burgers

Teriyaki Burgers

1 pound ground beef
2 tablespoons soy sauce
1 teaspoon salt
$1/4$ teaspoon crushed gingerroot or $1/8$ teaspoon ground ginger
1 clove garlic, crushed

Shape ground beef into 4 patties, each about $3/4$ inch thick. Mix remaining ingredients; spoon onto patties. Turn patties; let stand 10 minutes.

Grill patties about 4 inches from medium coals, turning once, until desired doneness, 7 to 8 minutes on each side for medium. Serve on toasted sesame seed buns if desired. **4 servings**

PER SERVING: Calories 230; Protein 21 g; Carbohydrate 1 g; Fat 16 g; Cholesterol 65 mg; Sodium 1100 mg

TO BROIL: Prepare patties as directed above. Set oven control to broil. Place patties on rack in broiler pan. Broil with tops about 3 inches from heat, turning once, until desired doneness, about 5 minutes on each side for medium. Serve on toasted sesame seed buns if desired.

Easy Flavor

If you would like to add a smoky taste to your food, but don't have a smoker, don't despair. Soak hickory, green hardwood or fruitwood chips in water for 30 minutes, drain and toss onto the coals and you've got smoke. You can add a different flavor and aroma by sprinkling the hot coals with soaked and drained dried herbs. Try fresh herbs and garlic cloves, too.

Grilled Hamburgers

Would you like more hamburgers? Double the recipe to make 8 hamburgers.

1 pound ground beef
3 tablespoons finely chopped onion, if desired
3 tablespoons water
$1/2$ teaspoon salt
$1/4$ teaspoon pepper

Mix all ingredients. Shape mixture into 4 patties, each about $3/4$ inch thick. Grill patties about 4 inches from medium coals, to desired doneness, 7 to 8 minutes on each side for medium. Brush barbecue sauce on patties before and after turning, if desired. **4 burgers**

PER SERVING: Calories 230; Protein 21 g; Carbohydrate 0 g; Fat 16 g; Cholesterol 65 mg; Sodium 320 mg

Hamburgers Supreme

2 tablespoons chopped onion
2 tablespoons water
1 pound ground beef
1 egg
$1/4$ cup catsup
$1/3$ cup fine dry bread crumbs
2 tablespoons finely chopped mustard pickle
1 tablespoon Worcestershire sauce
1 teaspoon salt
$1/4$ teaspoon pepper

Mix all ingredients. Shape mixture into 6 patties; chill thoroughly. Grill 4 inches from hot coals 6 minutes on each side. Serve in toasted hamburger buns, if desired. **6 burgers**

PER SERVING: Calories 205; Protein 15 g; Carbohydrate 9 g; Fat 12 g; Cholesterol 80 mg; Sodium 620 mg

Cheeseburgers Deluxe

Use a pan on the back of the grill to keep Mushroom Topping warm.

Mushroom Topping (below)
1½ pounds ground beef
½ cup shredded Cheddar cheese (2 ounces)
¼ cup dry bread crumbs
¼ cup water
1 teaspoon lemon pepper

Prepare Mushroom Topping; keep warm or reheat after grilling Cheeseburgers. Mix remaining ingredients. Shape mixture into 8 patties, each about 4 inches in diameter.

Grill patties about 4 inches from medium coals, turning once, until desired doneness, 7 to 8 minutes on each side for medium. Serve each with Mushroom Topping. Serve in hamburger buns if desired. **8 burgers**

PER SERVING: Calories 250; Protein 18 g; Carbohydrate 4 g; Fat 18 g; Cholesterol 55 mg; Sodium 150 mg

Mushroom Topping

8 ounces small mushrooms, cut into halves
¼ cup chopped green onions (with tops)
1 tablespoon chopped fresh parsley
2 tablespoons margarine or butter
Grated Parmesan cheese

Cook and stir all ingredients except cheese in 10-inch skillet until mushrooms are tender, 2 to 3 minutes; sprinkle with cheese.

Chile-Cheese Burgers

1½ pounds ground beef
1 small onion, finely chopped (about ¼ cup)
1 teaspoon chile powder
1 teaspoon Worcestershire sauce
¾ teaspoon salt
¼ teaspoon garlic salt
¼ teaspoon pepper
¼ teaspoon red pepper sauce
Dash ground red pepper (cayenne)
6 slices Cheddar cheese, 2 × 2 inches
2 tablespoons canned chopped green chiles

Mix all ingredients except cheese and chiles. Shape mixture into 12 thin patties, about 3½ inches in diameter. Place 1 cheese slice and 1 teaspoon chiles on each of 6 patties. Top with a remaining patty, sealing edges firmly. Broil or grill patties about 4 inches from heat, turning once, to desired doneness, 7 to 8 minutes on each side for medium. **6 burgers**

PER SERVING: Calories 290; Protein 24 g; Carbohydrate 1 g; Fat 21 g; Cholesterol 80 mg; Sodium 490 mg

Grilled Deviled Burgers

Sauerkraut gives a tangy, satisfying flavor to this different burger.

1 pound ground beef
1 can (4½ ounces) deviled ham
1 small onion, finely chopped (about ¼ cup)
¼ teaspoon salt
⅛ teaspoon garlic salt
⅛ teaspoon pepper
1 can (8 ounces) sauerkraut, drained
5 slices Swiss cheese, 3 × 3 inches

Mix all ingredients except sauerkraut and cheese. Shape mixture into 5 patties, each about ¾ inch thick. Grill patties about 4 inches from medium coals 3 minutes; turn patties and top each with sauerkraut and cheese slice. Grill to desired doneness, 2 to 4 minutes longer for medium. Serve on toasted rye or pumpernickel buns, if desired. **5 burgers**

PER SERVING: Calories 385; Protein 29 g; Carbohydrate 4 g; Fat 28 g; Cholesterol 100 mg; Sodium 890 mg

MICROWAVE DIRECTIONS: Prepare patties as directed above. Arrange patties on microwavable rack in microwavable dish. Cover with waxed paper and microwave on high 3 minutes; rotate dish ½ turn. Microwave until patties are almost done, 2 to 4 minutes longer. Pour off drippings.

Top each patty with sauerkraut and cheese slice. Microwave uncovered 1 minute; rotate dish ½ turn. Microwave until cheese begins to melt, 30 to 90 seconds longer. Serve on toasted rye or pumpernickel buns, if desired.

Blue Ribbon Burgers

2 pounds ground beef
2 teaspoons Worcestershire sauce
½ teaspoon salt
¼ teaspoon garlic salt
¼ teaspoon pepper
1 package (3 ounces) cream cheese, softened
2 tablespoons crumbled blue cheese
1 can (4 ounces) mushroom stems and pieces, drained and chopped

Mix meat, Worcestershire sauce and seasonings. Shape mixture into 12 thin patties, about 4 inches in diameter.

Mix cream cheese and blue cheese. Top each of 6 patties with cheese mixture, spreading to within ½ inch of edge; press mushrooms into cheese. Cover each with a remaining patty, sealing edges firmly. Broil or grill patties about 4 inches from heat, 7 to 8 minutes on each side for medium, turning once, to desired doneness.

6 large burgers

PER SERVING: Calories 370; Protein 30 g; Carbohydrate 2 g; Fat 27 g; Cholesterol 105 mg; Sodium 470 mg

Grilled Lamb Chops

The timetable will help you grill your chops just right.

Grilling Sauces (below and right)
1 to 2 loin, rib or shoulder lamb chops per serving

Prepare grilling sauce. Remove fell (the paperlike covering) if it is on chops. Slash outer edge of fat on lamb chops diagonally at 1-inch intervals to prevent curling (do not cut into lean).

Cover and grill lamb 5 to 6 inches from medium coals, turning and brushing 2 or 3 times with sauce, until done (see timetable). Serve with any remaining sauce. **4 servings**

PER SERVING: Calories 120; Protein 17 g; Carbohydrate 0 g; Fat 6 g; Cholesterol 55 mg; Sodium 45 mg

TO BROIL: Prepare lamb chops as directed above. Set oven control to broil. Place lamb on rack in broiler pan; place broiler pan so tops of 3/4- to 1-inch chops are 2 to 3 inches from heat, 1- to 2-inch chops are 3 to 5 inches from heat. Broil until brown. The chops should be about half done (see timetable).

Sprinkle brown side with salt and pepper if desired. (Always season after browning because salt tends to draw moisture to surface, delaying browning.) Turn chops; broil until brown.

Garlic Mint Sauce

1/2 cup mint-flavored apple jelly
2 tablespoons water
2 cloves garlic, crushed

Heat all ingredients over medium heat, stirring constantly, until jelly is melted.

Herbed Red Wine Sauce

1/4 cup dry red wine
1/4 cup chile sauce
1/4 teaspoon dried oregano leaves, crushed
1/4 teaspoon dried thyme leaves, crushed
1/4 teaspoon dried rosemary leaves, crushed

Mix all ingredients.

Orange-Ginger Sauce

1/4 cup frozen orange juice concentrate, thawed
1/4 cup soy sauce
1 teaspoon crushed gingerroot

Mix all ingredients.

Red Currant Sauce

1/2 cup red currant jelly
1 tablespoon prepared mustard
1 tablespoon soy sauce

Heat all ingredients over medium heat, stirring constantly, until jelly is melted.

TIMETABLE FOR BROILING OR GRILLING LAMB CHOPS

THICKNESS	APPROXIMATE TOTAL COOKING TIME*
3/4 to 1 inch	12 minutes
1 1/2 inches	18 minutes
2 inches	22 minutes

**Time given is for medium doneness (160°); lamb chops are not usually served rare.*

Leg of Lamb Barbecue

4- to 5-pound leg of lamb, boned
2 small cloves garlic, peeled and slivered
1/2 cup red wine vinegar
1/3 cup vegetable oil
1/3 cup packed brown sugar
2 tablespoons dried tarragon leaves
1 teaspoon salt
2 green onions (with tops), cut into 2-inch slices
1 can (8 ounces) tomato sauce

Trim excess fat from lamb; if necessary, cut lamb to lie flat. Cut 4 or 5 slits in lamb with tip of sharp knife; insert garlic slivers in slits. Mix remaining ingredients except tomato sauce; pour over lamb in glass dish. Cover and refrigerate, turning lamb 2 or 3 times, at least 8 hours.

Remove lamb; stir tomato sauce into marinade. Cover and grill lamb 5 to 6 inches from medium coals until done (175°), 50 to 60 minutes; turn lamb every 10 minutes and brush 2 or 3 times with marinade mixture during last 10 minutes of grilling. Remove garlic slivers. **14 servings**

PER SERVING: Calories 330; Protein 37 g; Carbohydrate 7 g; Fat 17 g; Cholesterol 120 mg; Sodium 350 mg

Lamb Chops with Pineapple

The fresh-tasting combination of mint and pineapple complements lamb beautifully.

3 tablespoons orange juice
2 tablespoons honey
4 lamb loin chops, 1 inch thick (about 1 pound)
1 1/2 cups cubed pineapple*
1 tablespoon chopped fresh or 1 teaspoon dried mint leaves

Mix orange juice and honey; reserve 2 tablespoons. Place lamb chops on grill. Cover and grill lamb 5 to 6 inches from medium coals about 12 minutes, turning and brushing with orange mixture once, until desired doneness.

Heat remaining orange mixture, the pineapple and mint to boiling, stirring occasionally. Serve with lamb chops. **4 servings**

PER SERVING: Calories 425; Protein 19 g; Carbohydrate 28 g; Fat 26 g; Cholesterol 85 mg; Sodium 50 mg

**1 can (20 ounces) pineapple chunks, drained, can be substituted for the fresh pineapple.*

Ground Lamb Kabobs

Ground Lamb Kabobs

These spiced minced-meat kabobs are grilled on skewers, then tucked into pita bread for serving.

1 1/2 pounds ground lamb
1 medium onion, chopped (about 1/2 cup)
1 cup chopped fresh parsley leaves
1 1/4 teaspoon salt
1/2 teaspoon coarsely ground pepper
1/2 teaspoon ground cumin
1/2 teaspoon paprika
1/4 teaspoon ground nutmeg
Vegetable oil
6 pita breads
2 medium tomatoes, chopped
4 green onions (with tops), sliced
Plain yogurt

Place lamb, chopped onion, parsley, salt, pepper, cumin, paprika and nutmeg in food processor workbowl fitted with steel blade; cover and process with about 20 on/off motions until mixture forms a paste.

Divide lamb mixture into 12 equal parts. Shape each part into a roll, 5 × 1 inch. (For easy shaping, dip hands in cold water from time to time.) Place 2 rolls lengthwise on each of six 14-inch metal skewers. Brush kabobs with oil.

Grill kabobs about 4 inches from medium coals, turning 2 or 3 times, until no longer pink inside, 10 to 12 minutes. Remove kabobs from skewers; serve on pita bread halves topped with tomatoes, green onions and yogurt.

6 servings

PER SERVING: Calories 455; Protein 24 g; Carbohydrate 31 g; Fat 26 g; Cholesterol 75 mg; Sodium 770 mg

Herbed Butterflied Leg of Lamb

If you have leftover marinade that you want to use as a sauce, heat it to boiling before serving.

2 tablespoons chopped fresh or 2 teaspoons dried rosemary leaves, crushed
3 large cloves garlic, finely chopped
2 tablespoons olive or vegetable oil
1 cup dry sherry or chicken broth
1 teaspoon salt
1/2 teaspoon pepper
3 1/2-pound butterflied leg of lamb

Cook rosemary and garlic in oil in 10-inch skillet, stirring frequently, until garlic is golden brown; remove from heat. Stir in sherry, salt and pepper. Place lamb in glass or plastic dish. Pour sherry mixture over lamb; turn lamb to coat. Cover and refrigerate at least 8 hours, turning lamb occasionally.

Remove lamb from marinade; reserve marinade. Cover and grill lamb 4 to 5 inches from medium coals 30 to 35 minutes for medium doneness, turning the lamb and brushing with marinade every 10 minutes. **9 servings**

PER SERVING: Calories 305; Protein 43 g; Carbohydrate 1 g; Fat 12 g; Cholesterol 150 mg; Sodium 230 mg

Grilled Pork Chops and Onions

4 pork loin or rib chops, each about ¾ inch thick
2 medium onions
2 teaspoons margarine or butter, melted
Salt to taste
Rubbed sage to taste
Pepper to taste

Grill pork and onions 4 inches from medium coals, turning 1 or 2 times and brushing onions with margarine, until pork is done (170°), about 20 minutes. Sprinkle salt and sage over onions; sprinkle salt and pepper over pork.

4 servings

PER SERVING: Calories 190; Protein 18 g; Carbohydrate 5 g; Fat 11 g; Cholesterol 60 mg; Sodium 70 mg

How to Marinate

Marinades are used to give special flavor to meats, poultry and fish. Many less tender cuts of meat also benefit from the tenderizing effects of marinating. Always marinate in a tightly covered *nonmetal* dish and turn the food occasionally with tongs. Plastic bags are also convenient for marinating. Just add the food and the marinade, and secure. Turn the bag now and then to redistribute the marinade. With either method, be sure to refrigerate the food while marinating for the length of time specified in the recipe.

Peanut Pork Chops

These stuffed pork chops are attractive to serve and very flavorful.

8 pork rib chops, about 1 inch thick
1 cup croutons
½ cup finely chopped salted peanuts
2 tablespoons instant minced onion
2 tablespoons finely chopped fresh parsley
½ to 1 teaspoon crushed red chile pepper
⅓ cup margarine or butter, melted
1 tablespoon water
¾ teaspoon salt
½ cup apple jelly
1 tablespoon lemon juice

Cut pocket in each pork chop on bone side.

Mix croutons, peanuts, onion, parsley and chile pepper in bowl. Mix margarine, water and salt. Pour over crouton mixture; toss. Stuff pork chop pockets with crouton mixture. Heat jelly and lemon juice just to boiling, stirring constantly.

Cover and grill pork 5 to 6 inches from medium coals until done and no longer pink in center (170°), 50 to 60 minutes; turn pork 3 or 4 times and brush with jelly mixture 2 or 3 times during last 30 minutes of grilling. **8 servings**

PER SERVING: Calories 345; Protein 20 g; Carbohydrate 19 g; Fat 21 g; Cholesterol 55 mg; Sodium 430 mg

Pork and Squash Kabobs

3/4-pound pork boneless top loin or tenderloin
2/3 cup apple butter
3 tablespoons vinegar
1 clove garlic, finely chopped
1 1/2 teaspoons chopped fresh or 1/2 teaspoon dried rosemary leaves, crushed
2 medium onions, cut into eighths
3 small (2 1/2 to 3 inches) pattypan squash, cut into fourths, or 12 one-inch pieces Hubbard squash

Trim excess fat from pork loin. Cut pork into 1 1/2-inch cubes. Mix apple butter, vinegar, garlic and rosemary in glass or plastic bowl. Stir in pork, coating evenly. Cover and refrigerate at least 6 hours. Remove pork from marinade; reserve marinade.

Thread pork alternately with onions and squash on four 11-inch metal skewers, leaving space between each piece. Brush kabobs with reserved marinade. Cover and grill kabobs 5 to 6 inches from medium coals 20 to 25 minutes, turning and brushing every 5 minutes with reserved marinade, until pork is no longer pink in center. **4 servings**

PER SERVING: Calories 275; Protein 13 g; Carbohydrate 28 g; Fat 13 g; Cholesterol 45 mg; Sodium 35 mg

Gingered Ham Slice

1/4 cup corn syrup
1/4 cup ginger ale
1 tablespoon crushed fresh gingerroot or 1/4 teaspoon ground ginger
1 can (15 1/2 ounces) sliced pineapple, drained
1 fully cooked smoked ham slice, 1 inch thick (about 2 pounds)

Mix corn syrup, ginger ale and gingerroot; reserve. Place pineapple in greased hinged wire grill basket.

Cover and grill ham 5 to 6 inches from medium coals, turning and brushing 2 or 3 times with reserved ginger mixture, until ham is done (140°), 20 to 25 minutes. Cover and grill pineapple, turning basket once and brushing pineapple 2 or 3 times with ginger mixture, until heated through, about 10 minutes. Brush ham with ginger mixture. Cut into serving pieces. Garnish with pineapple slices. **6 servings**

PER SERVING: Calories 345; Protein 34 g; Carbohydrate 21 g; Fat 14 g; Cholesterol 90 mg; Sodium 2280 mg

Barbecued Ribs

Barbecued Ribs

4½-pound rack fresh pork loin back ribs
3 cups water
½ cup soy sauce
1 tablespoon plus 1½ teaspoons cornstarch
Sweet and Sour Sauce (below)

Place pork back ribs in Dutch oven; add water. Heat to boiling; reduce heat. Cover and simmer 5 minutes. Remove ribs; drain. Mix soy sauce and cornstarch; brush on ribs. Continue brushing both sides of ribs with soy sauce mixture every 10 minutes, allowing mixture to penetrate pork, until mixture is gone.

Cover and grill ribs 5 to 6 inches from medium coals, brushing with Sweet and Sour Sauce every 3 minutes, until ribs are done and meat begins to pull away from bone (170°), 15 to 20 minutes. Cut into serving pieces. Serve with remaining sauce. **8 servings**

PER SERVING: Calories 425; Protein 21 g; Carbohydrate 20 g; Fat 29 g; Cholesterol 85 mg; Sodium 1790 mg

Sweet and Sour Sauce

1 cup water
1 cup ketchup
¼ cup packed brown sugar
¼ cup vinegar
¼ cup Worcestershire sauce
1 tablespoon celery seed
1 teaspoon chile powder
1 teaspoon salt
Few drops red pepper sauce
Dash of pepper

Heat all ingredients to boiling; remove from heat.

Franks on the Grill

Start with a basic, grilled frank, then have fun with the following variations.

Grill frankfurters 5 to 6 inches from medium coals, turning 4 or 5 times, until heated through, 12 to 15 minutes.

Franks and Onions

For each serving, fry 1 slice bacon 2 minutes on each side. Cut frankfurter lengthwise almost through to bottom; place 1 green onion in cut. Wrap frankfurter with bacon; secure with toothpicks.

Glazed Franks

For each serving, make diagonal cuts in frankfurter almost through to bottom. Mix 1 tablespoon packed brown sugar and 1½ teaspoons horseradish; brush on frankfurter.

Oriental Franks

For each serving, fry 1 slice bacon 2 minutes on each side. Cut frankfurter lengthwise almost through to bottom; place 3 mandarin orange segments in cut. Wrap frankfurter with bacon; secure with toothpicks.

PER SERVING: Calories 185; Protein 6 g; Carbohydrate 7 g; Fat 15 g; Cholesterol 25 mg; Sodium 580 mg

Italian Sausage Kabobs

Italian Sausage Kabobs

½ cup pizza sauce
1 tablespoon dried basil leaves
1 tablespoon vegetable oil
1½ pounds Italian-style sausage links, cut into 1½-inch pieces
2 medium zucchini, cut into 1-inch pieces
1 medium red bell pepper, cut into 1½-inch pieces
1 medium green bell pepper, cut into 1½-inch pieces
6 large pimiento-stuffed olives

Mix pizza sauce, basil and oil; reserve. Cook sausage pieces over medium heat until partially cooked, about 10 minutes; drain. Alternate sausage pieces, zucchini pieces and bell pepper pieces on each of 6 metal skewers, leaving space between foods. Place olive on tip of each skewer.

Cover and grill kabobs 5 to 6 inches from medium coals, turning and brushing 2 or 3 times with pizza sauce mixture, until sausage is done and vegetables are crisp-tender, 20 to 25 minutes. **6 servings**

PER SERVING: Calories 445; Protein 24 g; Carbohydrate 8 g; Fat 35 g; Cholesterol 90 mg; Sodium 1300 mg

TO BROIL: Set oven control to broil. Broil sausage pieces until partially cooked; prepare sauce and kabobs as directed above. Place kabobs on rack in broiler pan. Broil with tops about 5 inches from heat, turning and brushing 2 or 3 times with pizza sauce mixture, until sausage is done and vegetables are tender, about 15 minutes.

Apple-stuffed Chicken Breasts (page 25)

2

Poultry Greats

Barbecued Chicken

This fresh, homemade barbecue basting sauce not only flavors the chicken but helps keep it moist while grilling.

2½-pound cut-up broiler-fryer chicken
¾ cup tomato juice
1 small onion, finely chopped (about ¼ cup)
3 tablespoons lemon juice
2 tablespoons margarine or butter
1½ teaspoons Worcestershire sauce
1½ teaspoons paprika
½ teaspoon sugar
¼ teaspoon salt
¼ teaspoon pepper

Grill chicken, bone sides down, 5 inches from medium coals 20 to 30 minutes. Mix remaining ingredients in 1-quart saucepan. Heat just to boiling; keep hot. Turn chicken. Grill 30 to 40 minutes longer, turning and brushing frequently with sauce, until done. **6 servings**

PER SERVING: Calories 275; Protein 30 g; Carbohydrate 2 g; Fat 15 g; Cholesterol 100 mg; Sodium 250 mg

Herb-marinated Chicken

2½-pound cut-up broiler-fryer chicken
½ cup white wine or apple juice
1 small onion, grated
2 tablespoons vegetable oil
3 tablespoons chopped fresh or 1 tablespoon mixed dried herbs (basil, marjoram, thyme, rosemary, oregano)
1 tablespoon dry mustard
½ teaspoon garlic powder
½ teaspoon coarsely ground pepper
1½ teaspoons Worcestershire sauce
½ teaspoon soy sauce

Place chicken in shallow glass dish. Shake remaining ingredients in tightly covered container; pour over chicken. Cover with plastic wrap and refrigerate at least 4 hours but no longer than 24 hours, turning chicken occasionally.

Remove chicken from marinade; reserve marinade. Grill chicken, bone sides down, 5 inches from medium coals 20 to 30 minutes; turn chicken. Grill 30 to 40 minutes longer, turning and brushing frequently with marinade, until done. **6 servings**

PER SERVING: Calories 335; Protein 31 g; Carbohydrate 5 g; Fat 20 g; Cholesterol 100 mg; Sodium 135 mg

Pick-a-Sauce Grilled Chicken

If you aren't getting a sizzle as you grill, your coals may be too cool. To increase the heat, push coals closer together, lower the cooking surface or open the grill vents.

2½-pound cut-up broiler-fryer chicken
¼ teaspoon salt
¼ teaspoon pepper
Sweet and Sour Sauce, French Sauce or Hot Pepper Butter Sauce (below)

Sprinkle chicken with salt and pepper. Grill the chicken, bone sides down, 5 inches from medium coals 20 to 30 minutes; turn chicken. Grill 30 to 40 minutes longer, turning and brushing frequently with one of the sauces, until done. **6 servings**

PER SERVING: Calories 315; Protein 31 g; Carbohydrate 3 g; Fat 19 g; Cholesterol 100 mg; Sodium 350 mg

Sweet and Sour Sauce

Heat ½ cup chile sauce and ¼ cup plum or grape jelly over low heat, stirring constantly, until jelly is melted.

French Sauce

Mix 1 cup French dressing and 2 teaspoons celery seed.

Hot Pepper Butter Sauce

Mix ½ cup (1 stick) margarine or butter, softened, and ½ teaspoon red pepper sauce.

Grilled Chicken Fajitas

Slice onion crosswise but don't separate into rings—the onion will be easier to grill.

4 skinless boneless chicken breast halves (about 1 pound), cut into 4 × ¼-inch strips
1 medium onion, cut into ¼-inch slices
¼ cup lime juice
1 tablespoon vegetable oil
1 teaspoon chile powder
8 eight-inch flour tortillas
1 cup salsa
½ cup guacamole, if desired

Place chicken and onion in shallow glass or plastic dish. Mix lime juice, oil and chile powder; pour over chicken and onion. Cover and refrigerate 1 hour.

Remove chicken and onion from marinade; reserve marinade. Grill chicken and onion 4 to 6 inches from medium coals 8 to 10 minutes, brushing frequently with marinade, until chicken is done. Place chicken and onion on tortillas; fold. Top with salsa and guacamole.

4 servings

PER SERVING: Calories 355; Protein 32 g; Carbohydrate 42 g; Fat 7 g; Cholesterol 65 mg; Sodium 660 mg

Reheating Chicken in the Microwave

If you have leftover grilled chicken, cool quickly, cover and refrigerate, no longer than 3 or 4 days. To reheat, place 1 serving of refrigerated chicken on microwave-proof plate. Cover loosely and microwave on high until hot, 1 to 1½ minutes. Let stand 1 minute. For 2 servings, arrange pieces with thickest parts to edge of plate; microwave 2 to 3 minutes.

Chile Chicken

3/4 cup tomato and yellow chile sauce with onions
1 to 2 teaspoons chopped hot or mild green chiles
1 tablespoon chile powder
1 tablespoon vegetable oil
2 1/2-pound broiler-fryer chicken, cut into quarters

Mix all ingredients except chicken quarters. Cover and grill chicken, bone sides down, 5 to 6 inches from medium coals 20 to 35 minutes; turn and brush chicken with chile sauce mixture. Cover and grill, turning and brushing 2 or 3 times with chile sauce mixture, until chicken is done, 25 to 45 minutes longer. **4 servings**

PER SERVING: Calories 350; Protein 34 g; Carbohydrate 13; Fat 18 g; Cholesterol 105 mg; Sodium 650 mg

Chicken Afghanistan

3/4 cup plain yogurt
2 tablespoons lemon juice
1 tablespoon vegetable oil
1 teaspoon salt
1 clove garlic, crushed
1 teaspoon ground cumin
1 teaspoon ground ginger
1 teaspoon paprika
1 teaspoon almond extract
2 1/2-pound broiler-fryer chicken, cut up
1 lemon, thinly sliced
Paprika

Mix yogurt, lemon juice, oil, salt, garlic, cumin, ginger, 1 teaspoon paprika and the almond extract; pour over chicken pieces. Cover and refrigerate at least 1 hour.

Remove chicken; reserve marinade. Cover and grill chicken, bone sides down, 5 to 6 inches from medium coals, 15 to 30 minutes; turn chicken. Cover and grill, turning and brushing 2 or 3 times with reserved marinade, until chicken is done, 20 to 40 minutes longer. Sprinkle lemon slices with paprika; arrange on chicken.
6 servings

PER SERVING: Calories 225; Protein 24 g; Carbohydrate 3 g; Fat 13 g; Cholesterol 70 mg; Sodium 440 mg

Apple-stuffed Chicken Breasts

Soak toothpicks in cold water while you prepare the chicken for grilling. Wet toothpicks won't burn as quickly as dry ones will.

4 skinless boneless chicken breast halves (about 1 pound)
2 tablespoons sugar
1/4 teaspoon ground cinnamon
2 medium tart cooking apples, peeled and cut into thin slices
1 cup apple cider
1 tablespoon cornstarch

Place chicken breast halves between 2 pieces of waxed paper. Pound chicken to 1/8-inch thickness. Mix sugar and cinnamon. Coat apple slices with sugar mixture. Divide apples among chicken breast halves. Fold chicken around apples; secure with toothpicks.

Cover and grill chicken 4 to 6 inches from medium coals 20 to 25 minutes, turning after 10 minutes, until done. Remove toothpicks. Mix the apple cider and cornstarch in 1-quart saucepan. Cook over medium heat until thickened and bubbly. Spoon over chicken. **4 servings**

PER SERVING: Calories 230; Protein 26 g; Carbohydrate 27 g; Fat 2 g; Cholesterol 65 mg; Sodium 80 mg

Honey-glazed Chicken

½ cup honey
2 tablespoons vegetable oil
2 tablespoons prepared mustard
2 tablespoons lemon juice
½ teaspoon grated lemon peel
½ teaspoon salt
2½-pound broiler-fryer chicken, cut up

Mix all ingredients except chicken pieces. Cover and grill chicken, bone sides down, 5 to 6 inches from medium coals, 15 to 30 minutes; turn chicken. Cover and grill, turning and brushing 2 or 3 times with honey mixture, until chicken is done, 20 to 40 minutes longer. **6 servings**

PER SERVING: Calories 315; Protein 23 g; Carbohydrate 24 g; Fat 14 g; Cholesterol 70 mg; Sodium 300 mg

Herb-smoked Chicken

Smoked poultry is pinker in color than roasted poultry.

3 cups hickory wood chips
3-pound broiler-fryer chicken
½ teaspoon ground sage
½ teaspoon ground oregano
1 tablespoon dried tarragon leaves
1 tablespoon dried oregano leaves
1 tablespoon dried parsley flakes

Cover hickory chips with water. Let stand 30 minutes; drain.

Rub outside and cavity of chicken with sage and ground oregano. Flatten chicken wings over breast; tie with heavy string to hold securely. Tie legs together, then tie to tail. Insert spit rod through cavity from breast end toward tail; hold firmly in place with adjustable holding forks. Insert barbecue meat thermometer so tip is in thickest part of inside thigh muscle and does not touch bone.

Add 1 cup hickory chips to hot charcoal. Fill water pan with water. Add tarragon, oregano leaves and the parsley to water pan. Place chicken, breast side up, on rack about 6 inches from water pan over coals. Cover smoker and smoke-cook chicken, adding charcoal and soaked hickory chips every hour, until done (185°), 4 to 6 hours (add water to pan during cooking if necessary). **6 servings**

PER SERVING: Calories 220; Protein 27 g; Carbohydrate 1 g; Fat 12 g; Cholesterol 85 mg; Sodium 75 mg

Flatten chicken wings over breast; tie with heavy string to hold securely.

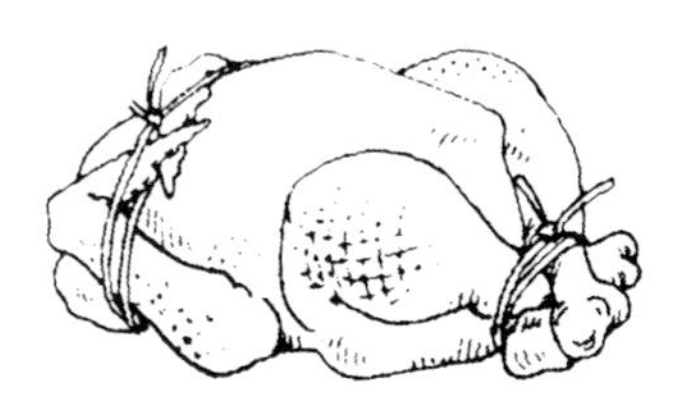

Tie legs together, then tie to tail.

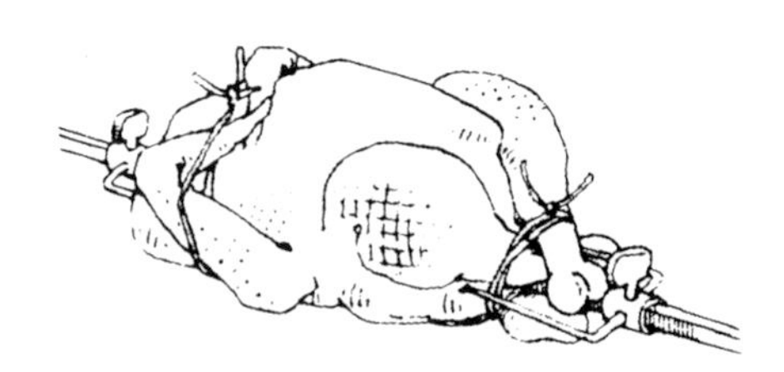

Insert spit rod through cavity of chicken from breast end toward tail; hold firmly in place with adjustable holding forks.

Honey-glazed Chicken

Grilled Chicken Breasts with Strawberry Butter

Fresh strawberry butter gives grilled chicken breasts a pretty color as well as wonderful flavor.

Strawberry Butter (below)
½ cup orange juice
¼ cup olive oil
½ teaspoon salt
¼ teaspoon pepper
10 skinless chicken breast halves (about 5 pounds)

Prepare Strawberry Butter. Mix orange juice, oil, salt and pepper in small bowl. Flatten each chicken breast between pieces of waxed paper to ½-inch thickness; place in shallow dish. Add orange juice mixture; cover and refrigerate 1 hour.

Remove chicken from marinade; drain. Grill chicken 5 to 6 inches from medium coals about 10 to 12 minutes, turning once. Serve chicken with Strawberry Butter. **10 servings**

PER SERVING: Calories 355; Protein 49 g; Carbohydrate 2 g; Fat 17 g; Cholesterol 125 mg; Sodium 250 mg

Strawberry Butter

1 cup strawberries
½ cup (1 stick) margarine or butter, softened
1 tablespoon grated orange peel

Place all ingredients in blender; cover and blend until mixed. (Mixture will not look smooth.)

Chicken and Rice

2 whole chicken breasts (about 1 pound), cut into halves
1 can (10¾ ounces) condensed cream of mushroom soup
⅔ cup uncooked instant rice
Paprika

Place each chicken breast on 14-inch square of double thickness heavy-duty aluminum foil. Mix soup and rice; spoon over chicken breasts. Sprinkle with paprika. Wrap securely in foil. Grill 5 inches from hot coals 20 minutes; turn once. Grill until chicken is done, 20 minutes longer. **4 servings**

PER SERVING: Calories 275; Protein 20 g; Carbohydrate 22 g; Fat 12 g; Cholesterol 50 mg; Sodium 660 mg

Chicken Cover-up

Covered cooking ensures even doneness. If your grill doesn't have a cover, improvise a cover or "tent" by loosely tucking heavy-duty foil over the food and the grill. Cover pieces of poultry, and you'll get moist insides with a golden brown, soft skin. Grilled uncovered, your poultry will be drier inside with a darker brown, crispier skin.

Grilled Chicken Adobo

The Achiote Sauce (right) makes more than enough for two recipes. Store the remainder in the freezer for a shortcut Chicken Adobo another time.

10 skinless boneless chicken breast halves (about 3½ pounds)
¼ cup Achiote Sauce (right)
1 cup orange juice
2 tablespoons lemon juice
2 tablespoons vegetable oil
1 teaspoon dried basil leaves
1 teaspoon ground cinnamon
½ teaspoon salt

Place chicken breasts in shallow glass or plastic dish. Mix remaining ingredients; pour over chicken. Cover and refrigerate 2 hours.

Remove chicken from marinade; reserve marinade. Cover and grill chicken 5 to 6 inches from medium coals 10 to 20 minutes.

Turn chicken. Cover and grill, turning and brushing with marinade 2 or 3 times, until done, 10 to 20 minutes longer.

Heat remaining marinade to boiling. Boil uncovered until thickened, 8 to 10 minutes. Serve with chicken. **6 servings**

PER SERVING: Calories 365; Protein 57 g; Carbohydrate 7 g; Fat 12 g; Cholesterol 145 mg; Sodium 310 mg

Achiote Sauce

⅓ cup achiote seeds (annatto seeds)
⅓ cup orange juice
⅓ cup white vinegar
1 teaspoon ground red chiles
½ teaspoon pepper
1 clove garlic

Cover achiote seeds with boiling water. Cover; let stand at least 8 hours. Drain seeds. Place seeds and remaining ingredients in food processor workbowl fitted with steel blade. Cover and process until seeds are coarsely ground; strain. Store in refrigerator up to 1 week or in freezer up to 2 months. **About ⅔ cup sauce**

BROILED CHICKEN ADOBO: Set oven control to broil. Remove chicken from marinade; reserve marinade. Place chicken in greased rectangular pan, 13 × 9 × 2 inches; pour half of the marinade over chicken. Broil chicken with tops about 4 inches from heat until light brown, about 10 minutes. Turn chicken; pour remaining marinade over chicken. Broil until done, about 6 minutes longer.

Grilled Tarragon Chicken Bundles

Grilled Tarragon Chicken Bundles

Add Potatoes in Foil (page 66) to the coals, and you have a complete meal on the grill.

6 skinless boneless chicken breast halves (about 1½ pounds)
6 medium carrots, cut lengthwise into quarters, then into 3-inch pieces
4 ounces mushrooms
6 small zucchini, cut lengthwise into quarters, then into 3-inch pieces
½ cup (1 stick) margarine or butter, melted
1 tablespoon chopped fresh tarragon leaves or 1 teaspoon dried tarragon leaves
1 teaspoon salt
¼ teaspoon pepper

Place chicken breast half on each of 6 pieces heavy-duty aluminum foil, 18 × 14 inches; top with vegetables. Drizzle with margarine; sprinkle with tarragon, salt and pepper. Wrap securely in foil.

Grill bundles 5 to 6 inches from hot coals until chicken is done and vegetables are tender, 45 to 60 minutes. **6 servings**

PER SERVING: Calories 325; Protein 27 g; Carbohydrate 12 g; Fat 19 g; Cholesterol 60 mg; Sodium 620 mg

TO BAKE: Bake bundles in shallow pan in 350° oven until chicken is done and vegetables are tender, 50 to 60 minutes.

Peanutty Chicken Kabobs

The unusual sauce for these kabobs comes from an old standby—the crunchy peanut butter in your cupboard.

1 pound skinless boneless chicken breast halves or thighs
⅓ cup crunchy peanut butter
⅓ cup boiling water
1 tablespoon grated gingerroot or 1 teaspoon ground ginger
1 tablespoon lemon juice
⅛ teaspoon crushed red pepper

Cut chicken into 1½-inch pieces. Mix remaining ingredients. Reserve ¼ cup. Thread chicken cubes on four 11-inch metal skewers, leaving space between each. Brush chicken with half of the reserved peanut butter mixture.

Cover and grill kabobs 4 to 5 inches from medium coals 15 to 25 minutes, turning and brushing with peanut butter mixture, until golden brown. **4 servings**

PER SERVING: Calories 215; Protein 21 g; Carbohydrate 5 g; Fat 12 g; Cholesterol 45 mg; Sodium 140 mg

Chicken with Pineapple

Chicken with Pineapple

1/4 cup dark rum or pineapple juice
1 tablespoon chile powder
1 tablespoon molasses
1/4 teaspoon red pepper sauce
4 chicken drumsticks
4 chicken thighs
Grilled Pineapple (below)

Mix all ingredients except chicken pieces and Grilled Pineapple; pour over chicken in glass dish. Cover and refrigerate at least 1 hour.

Remove chicken; reserve marinade. Cover and grill chicken, bone sides down, 5 to 6 inches from medium coals 15 to 20 minutes; turn chicken. Cover and grill, turning and brushing 2 or 3 times with reserved marinade, until chicken is done, 20 to 40 minutes longer. Serve with Grilled Pineapple. **4 servings**

PER SERVING: Calories 410; Protein 31 g; Carbohydrate 36 g; Fat 16 g; Cholesterol 105 mg; Sodium 120 mg

Grilled Pineapple

Cut off top of medium-size ripe pineapple. Cut pineapple lengthwise into 6 wedges; cut off pineapple core. Loosen fruit by slicing from rind (do not remove rind). Drizzle 1/4 cup honey over fruit; let stand 1 hour.

Grill pineapple, rind side down, 5 to 6 inches from medium coals, until heated through, 20 to 25 minutes.

Rotisserie Luau Turkey

1/4 cup pineapple juice
2 tablespoons soy sauce
2 tablespoons honey
1/2 teaspoon ground ginger
8- to 10-pound turkey

Mix all ingredients except turkey. Flatten turkey wings over breast; tie with heavy string to hold securely. Tie legs together, then tie to tail. Insert spit rod through cavity from breast end toward tail; hold firmly in place with adjustable holding forks.

Arrange hot coals around edge of fire box; place foil drip pan under grilling area. Cover and cook turkey on rotisserie about 4 inches from low heat until breast meat is white when pierced with knife (185°), 3 1/2 to 4 hours; brush turkey 2 or 3 times with pineapple juice mixture during last 30 minutes of cooking. Add coals during cooking to maintain even heat. Let turkey stand 15 minutes before carving. Garnish with sliced pineapple and mandarin orange segments if desired. **10 servings**

PER SERVING: Calories 580; Protein 72 g; Carbohydrate 5 g; Fat 30 g; Cholesterol 220 mg; Sodium 400 mg

Smoked Turkey

3 cups hickory wood chips
8- to 10-pound turkey
2 teaspoons poultry seasoning
1 onion, cut up
1 carrot, cut up
1 celery stalk, cut up

Cover hickory chips with water. Let stand 30 minutes; drain.

Rub outside and cavity of turkey with poultry seasoning. Place vegetables in cavity of turkey. Flatten turkey wings over breast; tie with heavy string to hold securely. Tie legs together, then tie to tail. Insert barbecue meat thermometer so tip is in thickest part of inside thigh muscle and does not touch bone.

Add 1 cup hickory chips to hot charcoal. Fill water pan with water. Place turkey, breast side up, on rack about 6 inches from water pan over coals. Cover smoker and smoke-cook turkey, adding charcoal and soaked hickory chips every hour, until done (185°), 7 to 8 hours (add water to pan during cooking if necessary). Let turkey stand 15 minutes before carving.

12 servings

PER SERVING: Calories 465; Protein 60 g; Carbohydrate 0 g; Fat 25 g; Cholesterol 185 mg; Sodium 160 mg

Parmesan Chicken Drumsticks

Substitute 2 teaspoons dried parsley flakes if you don't have fresh parsley on hand.

3/4 cup dry bread crumbs
1/2 cup grated Parmesan cheese
2 tablespoons chopped fresh parsley
1/2 teaspoon paprika
8 chicken drumsticks (about 2 pounds)
1 egg, beaten

Mix bread crumbs, cheese, parsley and paprika. Dip chicken drumsticks in egg; coat with bread crumb mixture.

Grill chicken 4 to 6 inches from medium coals 20 to 25 minutes, turning after 10 minutes, until done.

4 servings

PER SERVING: Calories 415; Protein 41 g; Carbohydrate 15 g; Fat 20 g; Cholesterol 200 mg; Sodium 480 mg

Cranberry-barbecued Chicken Wings

These flavorful chicken wings are so delicious you can easily make them your main course!

18 chicken wings (3½ to 4 pounds)
1 can (8 ounces) jellied cranberry sauce
1½ teaspoons packed brown sugar
1 teaspoon prepared mustard
1 teaspoon Worcestershire sauce

Place chicken wings in shallow glass dish. Mix remaining ingredients in 1-quart saucepan. Heat over low heat, stirring constantly, until smooth; pour over chicken. Cover and refrigerate at least 1 hour.

Remove chicken from marinade; reserve marinade. Cover and grill chicken 5 to 6 inches from medium coals 20 to 35 minutes, turning and brushing 2 or 3 times with marinade, until done. **18 chicken wings**

PER SERVING: Calories 185; Protein 14 g; Carbohydrate 4 g; Fat 12 g; Cholesterol 60 mg; Sodium 65 mg

Grilled Turkey Burgers

1 pound ground turkey
¼ cup dry bread crumbs
2 teaspoons instant minced onion
1 teaspoon prepared horseradish
½ teaspoon ground sage

Mix all ingredients. Shape mixture into 4 patties, each about 4 inches in diameter. Grill patties about 4 inches from medium coals, turning once, until desired doneness, 5 to 7 minutes on each side for medium. Serve in hamburger buns with cranberry relish if desired. **4 servings**

PER SERVING: Calories 220; Protein 23 g; Carbohydrate 5 g; Fat 12 g; Cholesterol 75 mg; Sodium 120 mg

Grilled Chicken Sandwiches

Grilled Chicken Sandwiches

1/2 cup white wine or apple juice
1 tablespoon chopped fresh parsley
1 teaspoon instant minced onion
1/2 teaspoon chopped fresh or 1/8 teaspoon dried thyme leaves
4 skinless boneless chicken breast halves (about 1 pound)
3 tablespoons mayonnaise or salad dressing
1 to 2 teaspoons prepared mustard
1 tablespoon chopped fresh parsley
1/2 teaspoon chopped fresh or 1/8 teaspoon dried thyme leaves
8 slices sandwich bread or 2 mini baguettes, split lengthwise into halves
Lettuce
1 tomato, cut into 8 slices

Mix wine, 1 tablespoon parsley, the onion and 1/2 teaspoon thyme; reserve. Cover and grill chicken 5 to 6 inches from medium coals 10 to 20 minutes; turn chicken. Cover and grill 10 to 20 minutes longer, turning and brushing 2 or 3 times with reserved wine mixture, until done.

Mix mayonnaise, mustard, 1 tablespoon parsley and 1/2 teaspoon thyme; spread on 4 slices bread. Top each with lettuce, 1 chicken breast half, 2 slices tomato and remaining bread. Cut diagonally into halves. **4 sandwiches**

PER SERVING: Calories 345; Protein 30 g; Carbohydrate 23 g; Fat 12 g; Cholesterol 70 mg; Sodium 350 mg

Grilled Turkey Legs

4 turkey drumsticks
1 tablespoon salt
1/4 cup soy sauce
2 tablespoons vegetable oil
1 tablespoon lemon juice
2 teaspoons crushed fresh gingerroot or 1 teaspoon ground ginger
1 teaspoon dry mustard
2 cloves garlic, crushed

Place turkey drumsticks and salt in Dutch oven; add enough water to cover. Heat to boiling; reduce heat. Cover and simmer until tender, 1 to 1 1/2 hours; drain.

Mix remaining ingredients; pour over turkey. Cover and grill turkey 5 to 6 inches from medium coals, turning and brushing 4 to 6 times with marinade, until turkey is done, 40 to 60 minutes. Cut turkey from bone to serve. **8 servings**

PER SERVING: Calories 215; Protein 29 g; Carbohydrate 0 g; Fat 11 g; Cholesterol 80 mg; Sodium 1000 mg

Turkey and Vegetables

Turkey and Vegetables

A hearty feast appropriate to serve year round.

8- to 10-pound turkey
2 teaspoons salt
¼ teaspoon ground red pepper (cayenne)
2 onions, cut into fourths
Vegetable oil
2 tablespoons margarine or butter, softened
½ teaspoon ground thyme
Roasted Potatoes (right)
Roasted Corn (right)
Roasted Tomatoes (right)

Rub cavity of turkey with salt and red pepper; place onions in cavity. Fold wings across back with tips touching. Tie legs together with heavy string, then tie to tail. Brush turkey with oil. Insert barbecue meat thermometer so tip is in thickest part of inside thigh muscle and does not touch bone.

Arrange hot coals around edge of firebox; place foil drip pan under grilling area. Mix margarine and thyme. Cover and grill turkey, breast side up, 5 to 6 inches from drip pan, brushing occasionally with thyme mixture, until breast meat is white when pierced with knife (185°), 3 to 4 hours. Add potatoes, corn and tomatoes as directed below. Add coals during cooking to maintain even heat. Let turkey stand 15 minutes before carving. Serve with Roasted Potatoes, Roasted Corn and Grilled Tomatoes.

12 servings

PER SERVING: Calories 755; Protein 60 g; Carbohydrate 48 g; Fat 36 g; Cholesterol 165 mg; Sodium 650 mg

Roasted Potatoes

Rub baking potatoes with margarine or butter, softened. Place on cooking grill. Cover and grill, turning once, until tender, 1 to 1½ hours.

Roasted Corn

Husk ears of corn and remove silk. Rub corn with margarine or butter, softened. Place on cooking grill. Cover and grill until tender, 25 to 35 minutes.

Grilled Tomatoes

Cut thin slice from stem ends of tomatoes. Sprinkle tomatoes with grated Parmesan cheese; dot with margarine or butter. Place tomatoes on cooking grill. Cover and grill until heated through, 10 to 15 minutes.

Fish Fillets with Flavored Butters

3

Sizzling Seafood

Fish Fillets with Flavored Butters

Flavored butters add lots of great taste without a lot of effort.

1½ pounds fish fillets, each ½ to ¾ inch thick
Flavored Butters (right)

Cover and grill fillets about 4 inches from medium coals, turning and brushing occasionally with one of the flavored butters, until fish flakes easily with fork, 15 to 25 minutes. Cut into serving pieces; top with a flavored butter.

6 servings

PER SERVING: Calories 95; Protein 21 g; Carbohydrate 0 g; Fat 1 g; Cholesterol 60 mg; Sodium 95 mg

MICROWAVE DIRECTIONS: Cut fish fillets into serving pieces. Place margarine for one of the flavored butters in square microwavable dish, 8 × 8 × 2 inches. Cover tightly and microwave on high until melted, 30 to 60 seconds. Stir in remaining ingredients for flavored butter.

Arrange fish, with thickest parts to outside edges, in dish; turn fish to coat well. Cover tightly and microwave 4 minutes; turn fish over and rearrange in dish. Cover tightly and microwave until fish flakes easily with fork, 3 to 5 minutes longer. Let stand covered 3 minutes.

Garlic Butter

2 tablespoons margarine or butter, softened
1 teaspoon chopped fresh or ½ teaspoon dried oregano leaves
½ teaspoon paprika
1 clove garlic, crushed
Dash of freshly ground pepper

Mix all ingredients.

Lemon Butter

2 tablespoons margarine or butter, melted
½ teaspoon grated lemon peel
1 tablespoon lemon juice
½ teaspoon Worcestershire sauce

Mix all ingredients.

Peppery Mustard Butter

2 tablespoons margarine or butter, softened
1½ teaspoons dry mustard
½ teaspoon lemon pepper

Mix all ingredients.

Grilled Fish Fillets with Shallot Sauce

1 1/2 pounds cod, haddock or halibut fillets, 1/2 to 3/4 inch thick
1/4 cup olive or vegetable oil
2 tablespoons lemon juice
1 teaspoon Dijon mustard
Shallot Sauce (right)

If fish fillets are large, cut into 6 serving pieces. Mix oil, lemon juice and mustard in shallow glass or plastic dish. Place fish in dish; turn to coat with marinade. Cover and refrigerate 1 hour.

Prepare Shallot Sauce. Grease hinged wire grill basket. Remove fish from marinade; reserve marinade. Place fish in basket. Grill fish about 4 inches from medium coals 8 to 12 minutes, brushing frequently with marinade and turning once, until fish flakes easily with fork. Serve with Shallot Sauce and, if desired, lemon wedges. **6 servings**

PER SERVING: Calories 270; Protein 23 g; Carbohydrate 1 g; Fat 19 g; Cholesterol 40 mg; Sodium 190 mg

Fish Grilling

A greased hinged grill basket is almost a necessity when grilling fish. It makes turning easier and keeps thin fillets and small pieces of fish from falling through the grill. If a basket is not available, brush the cooking grill with vegetable oil to help prevent the fish from sticking. Then, turn the fish only once.

Shallot Sauce

1/4 cup (1/2 stick) margarine or butter, melted
1 shallot, finely chopped
1 tablespoon finely chopped fresh parsley
1 tablespoon lemon juice

Heat margarine in 1-quart saucepan. Cook shallot in margarine over medium heat about 1 minute or until tender; remove from heat. Stir in parsley and lemon juice.

Orange-Honey Fish

2 tablespoons frozen orange juice concentrate, thawed
1 tablespoon soy sauce
1 tablespoon honey
1 tablespoon vegetable oil
1/2 teaspoon onion powder
1 pound cod, haddock or halibut fillets, 1/2 to 3/4 inch thick

Mix all ingredients except fish fillets; pour over fish in glass dish. Cover and refrigerate at least 1 hour.

Remove fish; reserve marinade. Cover and grill fish about 4 inches from medium coals, turning once and brushing 2 or 3 times with reserved marinade, until fish flakes easily with fork, 12 to 20 minutes. Cut into serving pieces if necessary. Garnish with orange slices if desired.

4 servings

PER SERVING: Calories 155; Protein 22 g; Carbohydrate 6 g; Fat 5 g; Cholesterol 60 mg; Sodium 350 mg

Teriyaki Fish

1½ pounds cod, haddock or halibut fillets, about 1 inch thick
¼ cup lemon juice
2 tablespoons soy sauce
1 tablespoon vegetable oil
2 cloves garlic, crushed

If fish fillets are large, cut into 6 serving pieces. Mix all ingredients except fish; pour over fish in glass dish. Cover and refrigerate at least 1 hour.

Remove fish; reserve marinade. Cover and grill fish about 4 inches from medium coals, turning once and brushing occasionally with reserved marinade, until fish flakes easily with fork, 12 to 20 minutes. Cut into serving pieces if necessary. Serve with lemon wedges if desired.

6 servings

PER SERVING: Calories 130; Protein 22 g; Carbohydrate 2 g; Fat 4 g; Cholesterol 60 mg; Sodium 440 mg

Lime Fish Fillets

Lime adds a fresh, southwest flavor to fish.

2 pounds fish fillets (bass, pike, mackerel or trout)
Vegetable oil
Paprika
½ cup (1 stick) margarine or butter, melted
¼ cup lime juice
Salt and pepper
Lime wedges

Brush fish with vegetable oil; sprinkle with paprika. Place fish in well-greased hinged wire basket or on well-greased grill 3 to 4 inches from medium coals. Cook, turning once, and brushing frequently with mixture of margarine and lime juice, until fish flakes easily with fork, 5 to 7 minutes. Sprinkle with salt and pepper; serve with lime wedges.

4 servings

PER SERVING: Calories 340; Protein 43 g; Carbohydrate 2 g; Fat 18 g; Cholesterol 120 mg; Sodium 320 mg

BACON-WRAPPED FISH FILLETS: Before grilling fish, place lime slices on side of fish; wrap fish and lime slices with bacon slices. Secure bacon with toothpicks.

Freezer-to-Grill Fish

A wonderful recipe for a night when you don't have time to defrost.

2 tablespoons lemon juice
2 tablespoons vegetable oil
1 tablespoon chopped chives
1 tablespoon chopped fresh parsley
½ teaspoon dried tarragon leaves
1 package (16 ounces) frozen fish fillets
2 medium tomatoes, cut into 6 slices
¼ cup shredded Cheddar cheese

Mix lemon juice, oil, chives, parsley and tarragon; brush on frozen block of fish. Reserve remaining mixture.

Cover and grill block of fish about 4 inches from hot coals, turning once and brushing occasionally with reserved lemon juice mixture, until fish flakes easily with fork, 20 to 30 minutes. Cut into serving pieces. Top each serving with tomato slice and about 2 teaspoons cheese. Serve on toasted English muffins if desired.

6 servings

PER SERVING: Calories 135; Protein 16 g; Carbohydrate 2 g; Fat 7 g; Cholesterol 45 mg; Sodium 100 mg

Grilled Swordfish

Anchovies and capers add Italian flavor to this swordfish.

1/2 cup olive oil
2 tablespoons capers, drained
2 tablespoons lemon juice
1 tablespoon chopped fresh parsley
1/2 teaspoon pepper
2 flat fillets of anchovy in oil
2 cloves garlic
4 swordfish steaks, about 1 inch thick (about 2 pounds)

Place all ingredients except swordfish steaks in food processor or in blender; cover and process until smooth. Place fish in ungreased rectangular baking dish, 12 × 7 1/2 × 2 inches. Pour oil mixture over fish. Cover and refrigerate 1 hour, turning fish after 30 minutes.

Grill fish uncovered about 4 inches from hot coals, turning once and brushing with marinade occasionally, 10 to 15 minutes or until fish flakes easily with fork. **4 servings**

PER SERVING: Calories 300; Protein 43 g; Carbohydrate 0 g; Fat 14 g; Cholesterol 120 mg; Sodium 75 mg

TO BROIL: Marinate fish as directed above. Set oven control to broil. Place fish on rack in broiler pan. Broil with tops about 4 inches from heat about 6 minutes; brushing fish with marinade frequently, until light brown. Turn carefully; brush with marinade. Broil 4 to 6 minutes longer, brushing with marinade, until fish flakes easily with fork.

Grilled Salmon with Mint Marinade

4 small salmon steaks, 3/4 inch thick (about 1 1/2 pounds)
1/2 cup chopped fresh mint leaves
1/2 cup olive oil
3 tablespoons lemon juice
1/2 teaspoon salt
1/2 teaspoon pepper
1 clove garlic, finely chopped
1 bay leaf

Place salmon steaks in ungreased rectangular baking dish, 11 × 7 × 1 1/2 inches. Beat remaining ingredients except bay leaf thoroughly; stir in bay leaf and drizzle over fish. Cover and refrigerate 1 hour, turning fish over after 30 minutes. Remove fish from marinade; reserve marinade.

Grill fish uncovered about 4 inches from hot coals, turning over once and brushing with marinade frequently, 10 to 15 minutes or until fish flakes easily with fork. Heat remaining marinade to rolling boil; remove bay leaf. Serve marinade with fish. **4 servings**

PER SERVING: Calories 365; Protein 36 g; Carbohydrate 1 g; Fat 24 g; Cholesterol 65 mg; Sodium 350 mg

TO BROIL: Marinate fish as directed above. Set oven control to broil. Place fish on rack in broiler pan. Broil with tops about 4 inches from heat about 5 minutes, brushing fish with marinade frequently, until light brown. Turn carefully; brush with marinade. Broil 4 to 6 minutes longer, brushing with marinade frequently, until fish flakes easily with fork.

Grilled Salmon with Mint Marinade

Monterey Fish Steaks

1½ pounds swordfish, halibut or salmon steaks, ¾ to 1 inch thick
1 teaspoon salt
¼ teaspoon pepper
¼ cup (½ stick) margarine or butter, melted
1 tablespoon lemon juice
1 teaspoon dried chervil leaves
Avocado Sauce or Caper Sauce (below)
Lemon wedges

Sprinkle fish steaks with salt and pepper. Mix margarine, lemon juice and chervil. Cover and grill fish about 4 inches from medium coals, turning once and brushing 2 or 3 times with margarine mixture, until fish flakes easily with fork, 15 to 25 minutes. Cut into serving pieces. Serve with Avocado Sauce or Caper Sauce and lemon wedges. **6 servings**

PER SERVING: Calories 185; Protein 21 g; Carbohydrate 0 g; Fat 11 g; Cholesterol 60 mg; Sodium 470 mg

Avocado Sauce

1 small avocado, cut up
⅓ cup sour cream
1 teaspoon lemon juice
¼ teaspoon salt
Few drops red pepper sauce

Beat all ingredients with hand beater until smooth.

Caper Sauce

1 lemon
¼ cup capers
1 tablespoon margarine or butter
1 tablespoon chopped fresh parsley
¼ teaspoon salt

Pare and chop lemon, removing seeds and membrane; mix with remaining ingredients. Heat until hot.

Grilled Garlic Halibut

Cilantro makes a nice contrast to the garlic—if you like spicy food, try adding a bit more red pepper.

2 tablespoons olive oil
¼ teaspoon salt
⅛ teaspoon ground red pepper (cayenne)
1 clove garlic, finely chopped
4 halibut steaks, 1 inch thick (about 1½ pounds)
Chopped fresh cilantro, if desired

Mix oil, salt, red pepper and garlic; spread on both sides of halibut steaks. Cover and grill on oiled grill 4 inches from medium coals 10 to 15 minutes or until fish flakes easily with fork. Sprinkle with cilantro. **4 servings**

PER SERVING: Calories 210; Protein 32 g; Carbohydrate 0 g; Fat 9 g; Cholesterol 90 mg; Sodium 270 mg

Fish Tips

Be careful—fish cooks quickly and extended cooking will toughen and dry it. For this reason, fish needs closer attention while grilling than other foods. Fish is fully cooked when the transluscent flesh becomes opaque and flakes easily with a fork. Cook all fish to an internal temperature of 175°, and use an "instant-read" thermometer to determine doneness.

Leftover fish that has been cooled quickly and refrigerated no longer than 3 days can be reheated in the microwave. For 1 serving, place refrigerated fish on a microwaveproof plate. Cover loosely and microwave on medium (50%) until hot, 1 to 1½ minutes. Let stand 1 minute. For 2 servings, microwave to 2½ minutes.

Grilled Tuna with Salsa

To seed tomatoes, cut into halves crosswise and squeeze gently—the seeds will be released easily.

3/4 cup finely chopped fresh parsley
1/4 cup finely chopped onion (about 1 small)
1/3 cup lemon juice
2 tablespoons vegetable oil
1/4 teaspoon salt
2 medium tomatoes, seeded and chopped
1 clove garlic, crushed
1 can (4 1/4 ounces) chopped black olives, drained
6 tuna or shark steaks (about 5 ounces each)

Combine all ingredients except tuna in glass bowl. Cover tightly and refrigerate salsa 2 to 4 hours to blend flavors.

Place tuna on oiled grill over medium-hot coals. Cook 3 minutes; turn steaks and cook 4 to 5 minutes or until tuna turns opaque in center. Remove from grill; keep warm. Serve with salsa. **6 servings**

PER SERVING: Calories 250; Protein 31 g; Carbohydrate 5 g; Fat 12 g; Cholesterol 85 mg; Sodium 320 mg

TO BROIL: Set oven control to broil. Arrange steaks on oiled rack in broiler pan. Broil with steaks about 4 inches from heat 10 to 15 minutes, turning after 6 minutes, until fish flakes easily with fork.

Spicy Breaded Red Snapper

1 pound red snapper or other lean fish fillets
1 1/2 cups seasoned croutons, crushed
1 teaspoon dry mustard
1/2 teaspoon salt
1/4 teaspoon ground red pepper (cayenne)
1/8 teaspoon pepper
1 egg
1 tablespoon water
3 tablespoons margarine or butter, melted

If fillets are large, cut into 4 pieces. Mix croutons, mustard, salt, red pepper and pepper. Beat egg and water until well blended. Dip fish into egg, then coat with crouton mixture.

Grease wire grill. Place fish fillets on grill. Grill 3 to 4 inches from medium coals 10 to 12 minutes, turning fish once and brushing with margarine, until fish flakes easily with fork. **4 servings**

PER SERVING: Calories 240; Protein 23 g; Carbohydrate 11 g; Fat 11 g; Cholesterol 100 mg; Sodium 595 mg

Grilled Red Snapper with Vegetable Sauté

Southwest Vegetable Sauté, including Lime Butter Sauce (below and right)
8 red snapper or cod fillets (about 5 ounces each)
1/4 cup vegetable oil
Salt and pepper

Prepare Southwest Vegetable Sauté and Lime Butter Sauce; keep warm. Generously brush fish fillets with oil; sprinkle with salt and pepper.

Grill over medium coals until fish flakes easily with fork, 10 to 12 minutes. Serve with Southwest Vegetable Sauté and Lime Butter Sauce. **8 servings**

PER SERVING: Calories 385; Protein 29 g; Carbohydrate 6 g; Fat 27 g; Cholesterol 160 mg; Sodium 400 mg

Southwest Vegetable Sauté

Lime Butter Sauce (right)
1 medium onion, finely chopped (about 1/2 cup)
2 cloves garlic, finely chopped
1/4 cup (1/2 stick) margarine or butter
4 very small pattypan squash (about 4 ounces each), cut into halves
2 small zucchini, cut into 1/4-inch strips
2 small yellow squash, cut into 1/4-inch strips
1 medium chayote, pared, seeded and cut into 1/2 inch cubes
1 small red bell pepper, cut into thin rings
1 small yellow bell pepper, cut into thin rings
1/2 teaspoon salt
1/4 teaspoon ground red pepper
8 fresh squash blossoms, if desired

Prepare Lime Butter Sauce; reserve. Cook and stir onion and garlic in margarine in 4-quart Dutch oven until onion is tender.

Stir in remaining ingredients except squash blossoms. Cook over medium heat, stirring occasionally, until vegetables are crisp-tender; stir in squash blossoms. Serve with Lime Butter Sauce.

Lime Butter Sauce

2 egg yolks
1 tablespoon lime juice
1/2 cup (1 stick) firm butter*
1/2 teaspoon grated lime peel

Stir egg yolks and lime juice vigorously in 1 1/2-quart saucepan. Add 1/4 cup of the butter. Heat over very low heat, stirring constantly, until butter is melted.

Add remaining butter. Continue heating, stirring vigorously, until butter is melted and sauce is thickened. (Be sure butter melts slowly so that sauce will thicken without curdling.) Stir in lime peel. Serve hot or at room temperature. Cover and refrigerate any remaining sauce.

**Margarine not recommended.*

Grilled Red Snapper with Vegetable Sauté

Fruit-stuffed Trout

4 pan-dressed rainbow trout (6 to 8 ounces each) or drawn trout (about 12 ounces each)
Fruit Stuffing (below)
2 tablespoons margarine or butter, melted
1 tablespoon lemon juice

Stuff fish with Fruit Stuffing. Close openings with skewers or wooden picks if necessary. Mix margarine and lemon juice. Drizzle over fish. Grease wire grill. Place stuffed fish on grill. Cover and grill about 4 inches from medium coals 12 to 15 minutes, turning fish once and brushing occasionally with margarine mixture, until fish flakes easily with fork. **4 servings**

PER SERVING: Calories 530; Protein 39 g; Carbohydrate 15 g; Fat 32 g; Cholesterol 100 mg; Sodium 315 mg

Fruit Stuffing

1 cup unseasoned croutons
1/3 cup diced dried fruits and raisins
2 tablespoons margarine or butter, melted
2 tablespoons dry white wine
1/4 teaspoon salt
1/8 teaspoon ground allspice
1 green onion (with top), chopped

Mix all ingredients until liquid is absorbed.

Stuffed Fish

8- to 10-pound salmon, cod or lake trout, cleaned
Salt
Pepper
Garden Vegetable Stuffing (below)
1/2 cup (1 stick) margarine or butter, melted
1/4 cup lemon juice
Vegetable oil

Sprinkle cavity of fish with salt and pepper; spoon Garden Vegetable Stuffing into cavity. Secure with skewers and lace with string.

Mix margarine and lemon juice; reserve. Brush fish with oil; place in hinged wire grill basket. Cover and grill about 4 inches from medium coals, turning basket 3 times and brushing fish occasionally with reserved lemon juice mixture, until fish flakes easily with fork, 45 to 60 minutes. **20 servings**

PER SERVING: Calories 340; Protein 39 g; Carbohydrate 3 g; Fat 19 g; Cholesterol 80 mg; Sodium 430 mg

Garden Vegetable Stuffing

1 large onion, finely chopped (about 1 cup)
1/4 cup (1/2 stick) margarine or butter
2 cups dry bread cubes
1 cup coarsely shredded carrot
1 cup chopped mushrooms
1 tablespoon plus 1 1/2 teaspoons lemon juice
1 egg
1 clove garlic, finely chopped
2 teaspoons salt
1/4 teaspoon dried marjoram leaves
1/4 teaspoon pepper

Cook and stir onion in margarine until onion is tender; toss with remaining ingredients.

Stuffed Fish

Grilled Seafood Kabobs

Marinade (right)
4-ounce salmon steak, cut into 1-inch cubes
4-ounce monkfish, cut into 1-inch cubes
4-ounce rockfish, cut into 1-inch cubes
12 medium raw shrimp in shells
8-ounce squid (calamari), cleaned, cut into 4 pieces
8 fresh large mushroom caps
1 large red bell pepper, cut into 1½-inch pieces
4 green onions (with tops), cut into 1-inch pieces
8 fresh or dried bay leaves

Prepare Marinade; reserve. Alternate fish, shrimp, squid, mushrooms, bell pepper, onions and bay leaves on each of four 12-inch metal skewers. Place kabobs in ungreased rectangular baking dish, 13 × 9 × 2 inches. Drizzle Marinade over kabobs. Cover and refrigerate 45 minutes. Remove kabobs from Marinade; reserve Marinade.

Grill kabobs uncovered about 4 inches from hot coals 10 minutes, turning once and brushing with reserved Marinade occasionally, until fish flakes easily with fork. Discard bay leaves.

4 servings

PER SERVING: Calories 240; Protein 31 g; Carbohydrate 7 g; Fat 10 g; Cholesterol 210 mg; Sodium 190 mg

Marinade

½ cup olive oil
1 tablespoon chopped fresh basil leaves
1 tablespoon chopped fresh parsley
3 tablespoons lemon juice
1 tablespoon capers, drained
1 teaspoon freshly ground pepper
½ teaspoon salt
1 green onion (with top), chopped

Place all ingredients in food processor or in blender; cover and process until smooth.

TO BROIL: Set oven control to broil. Place kabobs on rack in broiler pan. Broil with tops about 4 inches from heat 4 minutes, brushing with Marinade occasionally. Turn kabobs; brush with Marinade. Broil about 4 minutes longer, brushing with Marinade occasionally, until fish flakes easily with fork. Discard bay leaves.

Grilled Texas Shrimp

Shrimp cooks quickly, so keep a close eye on the grill.

1/4 cup vegetable oil
1/4 cup tequila or lime juice
1/4 cup red wine vinegar
2 tablespoons lime juice
1 tablespoon ground red chiles
1/2 teaspoon salt
2 cloves garlic, finely chopped
1 red bell pepper, finely chopped
24 large raw shrimp, peeled and deveined (leave tails intact)

Mix all ingredients except shrimp in shallow glass or plastic dish; stir in shrimp. Cover and refrigerate 1 hour.

Remove shrimp from marinade; reserve marinade. Thread 4 shrimp on each of six 8-inch metal skewers. Grill over medium coals, turning once, until pink, 2 to 3 minutes on each side.

Heat marinade to boiling in nonaluminum saucepan; reduce heat to low. Simmer uncovered until bell pepper is tender, about 5 minutes. Serve with shrimp. **6 servings**

PER SERVING: Calories 115; Protein 6 g; Carbohydrate 3 g; Fat 9 g; Cholesterol 55 mg; Sodium 240 mg

TO BROIL: Set oven control to broil. Place skewered shrimp on rack in broiler pan. Broil with tops about 4 inches from heat, turning once, until pink, 2 to 3 minutes on each side.

Garlic Shrimp

1/2 cup (1 stick) margarine or butter
2 teaspoons garlic salt
1/8 teaspoon red pepper sauce
3 pounds cleaned raw shrimp
1 can (8 ounces) sliced water chestnuts, drained
1 large green bell pepper, cut into rings
1 tablespoon finely chopped onion
1/2 teaspoon salt
1/2 teaspoon dried tarragon leaves

Form a pan, 11 × 11 × 1/2 inch, from double thickness heavy-duty aluminum foil. Place margarine, garlic salt and pepper sauce in pan; place on grill 4 to 6 inches from medium coals until margarine is melted. Remove pan from grill; add remaining ingredients. Cover pan with piece of heavy-duty aluminum foil, sealing edges well. Grill until shrimp is done, 20 to 30 minutes. **12 servings**

PER SERVING: Calories 160; Protein 17 g; Carbohydrate 3 g; Fat 9 g; Cholesterol 160 mg; Sodium 530 mg

Grilled Shrimp and Scallop Kabobs

Grilled Shrimp and Scallop Kabobs

You can also use bay scallops, as long as they are about 1 inch in diameter.

1/4 cup lemon juice
1/4 cup vegetable oil
1 tablespoon chopped fresh or 1 teaspoon dried thyme leaves
1/4 teaspoon salt
1/4 teaspoon pepper
3/4 pound sea scallops
12 raw large shrimp (in shells)
8 medium whole mushrooms (about 6 ounces)
8 cherry tomatoes
1 medium zucchini (about 1 inch in diameter), cut into 1-inch slices

Mix lemon juice, oil, thyme, salt and pepper. Cut scallops in half if over 1 inch in diameter. Arrange scallops, shrimp and vegetables alternately on four 10-inch metal skewers. Brush with lemon-thyme mixture. Grill 4 inches from medium coals 10 to 15 minutes, brushing with mixture frequently, until scallops are opaque in center and shrimp are pink. **4 servings**

PER SERVING: Calories 280; Protein 25 g; Carbohydrate 9 g; Fat 16 g; Cholesterol 65 mg; Sodium 400 mg

Grilled Marinated Vegetables (page 61)

4

Savory Marinades, Sauces and Vegetables

Ginger-Lime Marinade

This fresh, light marinade is great for fish, shrimp, chicken or pork.

1/4 cup lime juice
2 tablespoons olive or vegetable oil
1 teaspoon finely chopped fresh gingerroot
1/4 teaspoon salt
Dash of ground red pepper (cayenne)
1 clove garlic, crushed

Mix all ingredients in shallow glass or plastic bowl. Place seafood, poultry or meat in dish; turn to coat all sides with marinade. Cover and refrigerate at least 1 hour.

About 1/4 cup marinade

PER TABLESPOON: Calories 65; Protein 0 g; Carbohydrate 1 g; Fat 7 g; Cholesterol 0 mg; Sodium 140 mg

Cajun Marinade

A spicy blend that brings to mind Cajun cooking from New Orleans. Try it on vegetables, chicken and turkey.

1/4 cup dry sherry or chicken broth
1 teaspoon Worcestershire sauce
1/4 teaspoon ground red pepper (cayenne)
1/4 teaspoon black pepper
1/8 to 1/4 teaspoon red pepper sauce

Mix all ingredients in shallow glass or plastic dish. Place poultry or vegetables in dish; turn to coat all sides with marinade. Cover and refrigerate 1 hour.

About 1/4 cup marinade

PER TABLESPOON: Calories 10; Protein 0 g; Carbohydrate 2 g; Fat 0 g; Cholesterol 0 mg; Sodium 15 mg

Teriyaki Marinade

Try this Oriental marinade on turkey, pork, beef, chicken or lamb.

1/4 cup soy sauce
2 tablespoons water
1 tablespoon lemon juice
1 tablespoon vegetable oil
1 teaspoon packed brown sugar
1/8 teaspoon coarsely ground pepper
1 clove garlic, finely chopped

Mix all ingredients in shallow glass or plastic dish. Place meat or poultry in dish; turn to coat all sides with marinade. Cover and refrigerate at least 8 hours, turning occasionally.

About 1/2 cup marinade

PER TABLESPOON: Calories 25; Protein 0 g; Carbohydrate 2 g; Fat 2 g; Cholesterol 0 mg; Sodium 520 mg

Curry Marinade

An excellent choice for chicken, turkey, veal, pork or lamb.

1/2 cup orange juice
1/4 cup peanut butter
2 teaspoons curry powder

Mix all ingredients in medium glass or plastic dish. Place meat or poultry in dish; Turn to coat all sides with marinade. Cover and refrigerate 1 hour.

About 2/3 cup marinade

PER TABLESPOON: Calories 45; Protein 2 g; Carbohydrate 3 g; Fat 3 g; Cholesterol 0 mg; Sodium 30 mg

Brandy Marinade

A robust marinade for beef, pork and lamb.

1/3 cup brandy, bourbon whiskey or beef broth
1/3 cup soy sauce
2 tablespoons packed brown sugar
2 tablespoons vinegar
2 tablespoons vegetable oil
1/2 teaspoon pepper
1 small onion, chopped (about 1/4 cup)
1 clove garlic, finely chopped

Mix all ingredients in shallow glass or plastic dish. Place meat in dish; turn to coat all sides with marinade. Cover and refrigerate at least 24 hours, turning meat occasionally.

About 1 cup marinade

PER TABLESPOON: Calories 30; Protein 0 g; Carbohydrate 3 g; Fat 2 g; Cholesterol 0 mg; Sodium 340 mg

Make Your Own Marinades

Try these combinations for easy marinades.

Fresh lemon juice: Combine with oil and herbs.

Soy sauce: Combine with honey, garlic, herbs—or use alone.

Tomato juice or sauce: Combine with soy sauce, garlic, oil and seasonings. This is particularly good on very tough meat.

Vinegar: Combine with oil and herbs to make a vinaigrette. If you're pressed for time, try bottled vinaigrette.

Wine: In general, red wine is used, and combined with oil, spices and garlic.

Lemon Sauce

1/2 cup (1 stick) margarine or butter
1/2 clove garlic, crushed
2 teaspoons all-purpose flour
1/3 cup water
3 tablespoons lemon juice
1 1/2 teaspoons sugar
1 teaspoon salt
1/8 teaspoon pepper
1/8 teaspoon poultry seasoning
1/8 teaspoon red pepper sauce

Heat margarine in small saucepan until melted. Add garlic; cook and stir a few minutes. Stir in flour; cook over low heat, stirring until mixture is bubbly. Remove from heat. Add remaining ingredients; cook over medium heat, stirring constantly, until mixture thickens and boils. Cool and refrigerate. Brush on chicken or fish during last half of cooking period. **1 cup sauce**

PER TABLESPOON: Calories 60; Protein 0 g; Carbohydrate 1 g; Fat 6 g; Cholesterol 0 mg; Sodium 200 mg

Chef's Special Sauce

1/4 cup prepared mustard
1/4 cup pineapple juice
2 tablespoons packed brown sugar
1/2 teaspoon prepared horseradish
Dash of salt

Mix all ingredients. Heat in saucepan on grill; brush on pork or ham during last 15 minutes of cooking. Serve remaining sauce with meat.

1/2 cup sauce

PER TABLESPOON: Calories 20; Protein 0 g; Carbohydrate 5 g; Fat 0 g; Cholesterol 0 mg; Sodium 120 mg

Barbecue Sauce

Great on chicken or beef.

1 cup ketchup
1/2 cup finely chopped onion (about 1 medium)
1/3 cup water
1/4 cup (1/2 stick) margarine or butter
1 tablespoon paprika
1 teaspoon packed brown sugar
1/4 teaspoon pepper
2 tablespoons lemon juice
1 tablespoon Worcestershire sauce

Heat all ingredients except lemon juice and Worcestershire sauce to boiling over medium heat. Stir in lemon juice and Worcestershire sauce. Heat until hot.

About 2 cups sauce

PER TABLESPOON: Calories 25; Protein 0 g; Carbohydrate 3 g; Fat 1 g; Cholesterol 0 mg; Sodium 120 mg

Spicy Barbecue Sauce

1/3 cup margarine or butter
2 tablespoons water
2 tablespoons vinegar
1 tablespoon Worcestershire sauce
1 teaspoon sugar
1 teaspoon onion salt
1/2 teaspoon garlic powder
1/2 teaspoon pepper
Dash of ground pepper (cayenne)

Heat all ingredients, stirring frequently, until margarine is melted. **About 3/4 cup sauce**

PER TABLESPOON: Calories 50; Protein 0 g; Carbohydrate 1 g; Fat 5 g; Cholesterol 0 mg; Sodium 200 mg

Horseradish Sauce

A zesty sauce for beef.

½ cup mayonnaise or salad dressing
¼ cup sour cream
2 tablespoons prepared horseradish, well drained
2 tablespoons chopped fresh parsley
½ teaspoon salt

Mix all ingredients; cover and refrigerate at least 1 hour. **½ cup sauce**

PER TABLESPOON: Calories 110; Protein 0 g; Carbohydrate 1 g; Fat 12 g; Cholesterol 15 mg; Sodium 220 mg

Smoky Sauce

1 teaspoon packed brown sugar
¾ teaspoon salt
½ teaspoon prepared mustard
¼ teaspoon pepper
¼ cup water
2 tablespoons vinegar
2 tablespoons margarine or butter
1 thin slice lemon
1 slice onion
¼ cup ketchup
1 tablespoon Worcestershire sauce
¾ teaspoon liquid smoke

Mix all ingredients except ketchup, Worcestershire sauce and liquid smoke in small saucepan. Heat to boiling. Reduce heat and simmer uncovered 20 minutes; strain. Stir in remaining ingredients. Heat to boiling. Baste beef during last half of grilling period. **¾ cup sauce**

PER TABLESPOON: Calories 25; Protein 0 g; Carbohydrate 2 g; Fat 2 g; Cholesterol 0 mg; Sodium 230 mg

Salsa

3 medium tomatoes, seeded and chopped (about 3 cups)
½ cup sliced green onions (with tops)
½ cup chopped green bell pepper
2 to 3 tablespoons lime juice
2 tablespoons chopped fresh cilantro leaves
1 tablespoon finely chopped jalapeño chiles
½ teaspoon salt
3 cloves garlic, finely chopped

Mix all ingredients. **About 3½ cups**

PER TABLESPOON: Calories 2; Protein 0 g; Carbohydrate 1 g; Fat 0 g; Cholesterol 0 mg; Sodium 10 mg

Kabob Success Tips

- Soak bamboo skewers in water at least 30 minutes to prevent burning.
- Leave a little space between foods threaded on skewers—tightly packed food will not cook evenly.
- Be sure coals aren't too hot or too cold. If you can hold your hand, palm down, near the cooking surface for 4 to 5 seconds, the coals have reached medium heat.
- To prevent sticking (and to make cleanup easier), brush cooking surface with vegetable oil before grilling.
- Sauces that contain sugar burn easily. Brush them on kabobs only during last 15 minutes of grilling.
- To avoid food-borne illnesses caused by eating undercooked or raw meat, boil the sauce you've dipped your basting brush into before serving with cooked kabobs.

Grilled Marinated Vegetables

Grilltop screens or racks help keep small pieces of food, such as cut-up vegetables, from falling onto the coals.

6 pattypan squash (about 2 inches in diameter)
3 zucchini or yellow squash, cut lengthwise into halves
1 red or green bell pepper, cut into 6 pieces
1 large red onion, cut into 1/2-inch slices
1/3 cup olive or vegetable oil
1 tablespoon lemon juice
1 1/2 teaspoons chopped fresh or 1/2 teaspoon dried marjoram leaves
1 clove garlic, crushed
1/4 teaspoon salt
1/8 teaspoon pepper

Arrange vegetables in rectangular baking dish, 13 × 9 × 2 inches. Mix oil, lemon juice, marjoram and garlic; pour over vegetables. Cover and let stand at least 1 hour.

Remove vegetables from marinade; reserve marinade. Cover and grill vegetables 4 inches from medium coals 10 to 15 minutes, turning and brushing 2 or 3 times with marinade, until golden brown and tender. Sprinkle with the salt and pepper. **6 servings**

PER SERVING: Calories 145; Protein 2 g; Carbohydrate 9 g; Fat 12 g; Cholesterol 0 mg; Sodium 95 mg

Grilled Summer Squash

2 medium zucchini
2 medium yellow squash
24 small pattypan squash or cherry tomatoes
1/4 cup olive oil
Dill Butter (below)

Cut zucchini and yellow squash into 1-inch pieces. Thread squash, zucchini and tomatoes onto 10-inch metal skewers; brush with olive oil. Grill 5 to 6 inches from medium coals about 8 minutes, turning several times, until squash is tender. Serve with Dill Butter. **8 servings**

PER SERVING: Calories 245; Protein 5 g; Carbohydrate 13 g; Fat 19 g; Cholesterol 30 mg; Sodium 90 mg

Dill Butter

1/2 cup (1 stick) margarine or butter
3 tablespoons chopped fresh or 1 tablespoon dried dill weed

Mix margarine and dill weed until well blended.

Grilled Eggplant

1/3 cup vegetable oil
2 tablespoons lemon juice
2 cloves garlic, crushed
2 teaspoons dried oregano leaves, crushed
1 teaspoon salt
2 medium eggplants (about 2 1/2 pounds)
1 cup shredded mozzarella cheese (about 4 ounces)

Mix all ingredients except eggplants and cheese. Cut eggplants into 1 1/2-inch slices; dip in oil mixture, coating both sides. Cover and grill eggplants 5 to 6 inches from medium coals until tender, 8 to 12 minutes; turn and brush eggplants 2 or 3 times with oil mixture and top with cheese during last 2 minutes of grilling.

8 servings

PER SERVING: Calories 170; Protein 5 g; Carbohydrate 10 g; Fat 12 g; Cholesterol 10 mg; Sodium 350 mg

Grilled Eggplant Dip

Tahini is a thick paste made from ground sesame seed.

1 medium eggplant (about 2 pounds)
4 to 5 tablespoons lemon juice
1/4 cup sesame seed paste (tahini)
1 teaspoon salt
2 cloves garlic, crushed
2 teaspoons olive or vegetable oil
Paprika

Pierce eggplant in several places with long-tined fork. Cover and grill eggplant about 4 inches from medium coals 20 to 30 minutes, turning frequently, until eggplant is very soft and the skin is charred. Place eggplant in a wire colander about 30 minutes to drain and cool.

Cut eggplant lengthwise in half. Scoop out and finely chop the pulp. Mix eggplant, lemon juice, sesame seed paste, salt and garlic. Spoon eggplant mixture into a shallow serving bowl; flatten top of mixture with back of spoon. Carefully drizzle oil over top; sprinkle with paprika. Serve with breadsticks, crackers or toasted pita bread wedges if desired.

1 1/2 cups dip

PER SERVING: Calories 30; Protein 1 g; Carbohydrate 3 g; Fat 2 g; Cholesterol 0 mg; Sodium 95 mg

Grilled Eggplant Dip

Grilled Zucchini with Basil

1/4 cup olive oil
2 tablespoons chopped fresh or 2 teaspoons dried basil leaves
1/4 teaspoon salt
1/4 teaspoon pepper
6 medium zucchini, cut into halves lengthwise

Mix all ingredients except zucchini. Place zucchini cut side up on grill 5 to 6 inches from medium coals; brush with oil mixture. Grill about 3 to 5 minutes until slightly soft. Turn zucchini over; brush with oil mixture and grill 2 minutes until tender. **6 servings**

PER SERVING: Calories 115; Protein 2 g; Carbohydrate 6 g; Fat 9 g; Cholesterol 0 mg; Sodium 95 mg

TO BROIL: Set oven control to broil. Arrange zucchini on rack in broiler pan; brush with oil mixture. Broil with zucchini 4 inches from heat 3 to 5 minutes. Turn over; brush with oil mixture and broil about 2 minutes until tender.

Spicy Grilled Corn

Try different twists on this easy corn-on-the-cob side dish. Omit the taco seasoning and substitute any fresh herb or grated orange or lemon peel, adjusting the amount to suit your taste.

4 ears corn
2 tablespoons margarine or butter
1 tablespoon taco seasoning mix or lemon pepper
2 tablespoons water

Husk ears and remove silk. Mix margarine and taco seasoning mix. Spread over corn. Place each ear on double thickness heavy-duty aluminum foil. Sprinkle ears with water. Wrap securely in foil and twist ends. Place ears on medium coals. Cover and grill 15 to 25 minutes, turning once, until tender. **4 servings**

PER SERVING: Calories 145; Protein 3 g; Carbohydrate 22 g; Fat 7 g; Cholesterol 0 mg; Sodium 340 mg

CORN IN THE HUSK: Omit water. Remove large outer husks. Turn back inner husks and remove silk. Spread margarine mixture over corn. Pull husks back over ears, tying with fine wire. Cover and grill corn 3 inches from medium coals 15 to 25 minutes, turning frequently, until tender.

Vegetable Kabobs

1½ pounds zucchini (about 3 medium), cut into ¾-inch slices
2 green bell peppers, cut into 1½-inch pieces
18 cherry tomatoes
18 whole mushrooms
½ cup Italian dressing
1 teaspoon garlic salt

Alternate vegetables on each of 6 metal skewers, leaving space between vegetables. Mix dressing and garlic salt; brush on vegetables.

Cover and grill kabobs 5 to 6 inches from medium coals, turning and brushing 2 or 3 times with dressing mixture, until vegetables are crisp-tender, 10 to 15 minutes. **6 servings**

PER SERVING: Calories 145; Protein 3 g; Carbohydrate 11g; Fat 10 g; Cholesterol 0 mg; Sodium 330 mg

SMOKY VEGETABLE KABOBS: Cover 1 cup hickory chips with water. Let stand 30 minutes; drain. Add hickory chips to hot coals. Continue as directed.

Pea Pod Packets

2 packages (6 ounces each) frozen Chinese pea pods
1 can (8 ounces) sliced water chestnuts, drained
2 tablespoons soy sauce
1 teaspoon sugar
½ teaspoon onion powder

Rinse frozen pea pods under running cold water to separate; drain. Place pea pods on 18-inch square of double thickness heavy-duty aluminum foil. Top with remaining ingredients; toss. Wrap securely in foil. Cover and grill packet 5 to 6 inches from medium coals, turning 2 or 3 times, until pea pods are hot and crisp-tender, 15 to 20 minutes. **6 servings**

PER SERVING: Calories 50; Protein 2 g; Carbohydrate 10 g; Fat 0 g; Cholesterol 0 mg; Sodium 350 mg

Grilled Onions

4 medium yellow onions, (unpeeled)

Grill onions 4 inches from medium coals 25 to 30 minutes, turning occasionally, until tender. Carefully remove skins from onions.

4 servings

PER SERVING: Calories 45; Protein 1 g; Carbohydrate 10 g; Fat 0 g; Cholesterol 0 mg; Sodium 00 mg

Grilled Mushrooms with Herbs

After standing for an hour, the mushrooms will have absorbed most, if not all, of the marinade.

1/2 cup olive or vegetable oil
3 tablespoons lemon juice
1/4 teaspoon dried oregano leaves
1 teaspoon chopped fresh or 1/4 teaspoon dried thyme leaves
1 clove garlic, crushed
1 pound very large mushrooms (about 2 1/2 inches in diameter)
1/4 teaspoon salt
1/8 teaspoon pepper

Mix oil, lemon juice, oregano, thyme and garlic in large glass or plastic bowl. Add mushrooms; stir to coat with marinade. Cover and let stand 1 hour.

Remove mushrooms from marinade. Cover and grill mushrooms about 4 inches from medium coals 15 to 20 minutes, turning 2 to 3 times, until tender and golden brown. Sprinkle with salt and pepper. **4 servings**

PER SERVING: Calories 90; Protein 2 g; Carbohydrate 6 g; Fat 7 g; Cholesterol 0 mg; Sodium 140 mg

Peas Almondine

2 packages (10 ounces each) frozen green peas
1/3 cup slivered almonds
2 tablespoons margarine or butter
Salt and pepper
1 tablespoon chopped pimiento

Place frozen blocks of peas side by side on 18-inch square of double thickness heavy-duty aluminum foil. Top with almonds, margarine, salt and pepper. Wrap securely in foil. Cover and grill packet 3 to 4 inches from medium coals, turning once, until tender, 25 to 30 minutes. Add pimiento just before serving. **6 servings**

PER SERVING: Calories 145; Protein 5 g; Carbohydrates 13 g; Fat 8 g; Cholesterol 0 mg; Sodium 300 mg

Potatoes in Foil

Choose medium sweet potatoes, yams or white baking potatoes. For each serving, scrub 1 potato and rub skin with vegetable oil, margarine or butter. Wrap potato securely in heavy-duty aluminum foil. Cover and cook potato on medium coals, turning 4 or 5 times, until tender (potato will be soft when pierced with fork), 45 to 60 minutes. Or, cover and grill potato 5 to 6 inches from hot coals, turning 4 or 5 times, until tender, 1 to 2 hours. Cut crisscross gashes through foil and into potato; fold foil back. Squeeze potato gently until some potato pops up through opening. Serve with margarine, butter or sour cream if desired.

PER SERVING: Calories 215; Protein 3 g; Carbohydrate 31 g; Fat 9 g; Cholesterol 0 mg; Sodium 10 mg

Zesty Grilled Potatoes

4 medium potatoes
1/2 cup Italian dressing

Heat 1 inch salted water (1 1/2 teaspoon salt to 1 cup water) to boiling. Add potatoes. Heat to boiling; reduce heat. Cover and cook until tender, 20 to 25 minutes; drain. While warm, cut potatoes diagonally into 1/2-inch slices; pour Italian dressing over hot slices. Let stand, turning potatoes once, 1 hour.

Remove potatoes. Arrange potatoes in hinged wire grill basket. Cover and grill 5 to 6 inches from medium coals, turning basket 2 or 3 times, until potatoes are golden brown, 20 to 25 minutes. Sprinkle with salt and pepper.

6 servings

PER SERVING: Calories 190; Protein 2 g; Carbohydrate 23 g; Fat 10 g; Cholesterol 0 mg; Sodium 340 mg

Spicy Grilled Potato Planks

Garam masala *is an Indian spice mixture. While it has no definite formula, it usually consists of cardamom, cinnamon and cloves. It might also include coriander, cumin, nutmeg, mace or pepper. Look for* garam masala *in health-food stores.*

3 medium potatoes (about 1 1/2 pounds)
1/2 cup (1 stick) margarine or butter
1/2 teaspoon salt
1/8 teaspoon ground red pepper (cayenne)
1/8 teaspoon garam masala, if desired
1 large clove garlic, crushed

Place potatoes in enough water to cover (salted if desired) in 3-quart saucepan. Cover and heat to boiling. Boil about 15 minutes or until almost tender; drain. Cool slightly.

Heat remaining ingredients to boiling; remove from heat. Cut each potato lengthwise into 4 or 5 slices. Brush potatoes generously with margarine mixture. Cover and grill potatoes 4 inches from medium coals about 20 minutes, turning and brushing 2 or 3 times with margarine mixture, until golden brown and tender.

4 servings

PER SERVING: Calories 330; Protein 3 g; Carbohydrate 30 g; Fat 23 g; Cholesterol 0 mg; Sodium 550 mg

Grilled Shortcake (page 75)

5

Breads and Desserts

Hickory Cheese Bread

Popular with cheese lovers.

1 loaf (1 pound) French Bread
½ cup (1 stick) margarine or butter, softened
1 cup shredded natural sharp Cheddar cheese (4 ounces)
1 tablespoon chopped fresh parsley
½ teaspoon hickory-smoked salt
2 teaspoons Worcestershire sauce

Cut bread diagonally into 1-inch slices, cutting almost to bottom of loaf. Mix remaining ingredients; spread between slices of bread. Place bread on 28 × 18-inch piece of heavy-duty aluminum foil; wrap securely. Cover and grill bread 5 to 6 inches from medium coals, turning once, until hot, 15 to 20 minutes. **24 slices**

PER SERVING: Calories 110; Protein 3 g; Carbohydrate 11 g; Fat 6 g; Cholesterol 5 mg; Sodium 220 mg

Grilled Texas Toast

¼ cup (½ stick) margarine or butter, softened
4 slices thick-cut white bread, about 1 inch thick
½ teaspoon seasoned salt

Spread margarine on both sides of bread slices. Sprinkle with seasoned salt. Grill bread 4 inches from medium coals 4 to 6 minutes, turning once, until golden brown. **4 servings**

PER SERVING: Calories 260 g; Protein 5 g; Carbohydrate 31 g; Fat 13 g; Cholesterol 0 mg; Sodium 610 mg

Cheese Loaf

Check to be certain grill height and heat are appropriate when two or more foods are grilled together.

1 loaf (1 pound) French bread
1 package (3 ounces) cream cheese, softened
1 cup shredded mozzarella cheese (4 ounces)
¼ cup chopped green onions (with tops)
2 tablespoons margarine or butter, softened
½ teaspoon garlic salt

Cut bread diagonally into 1-inch slices, cutting almost to bottom of loaf. Mix remaining ingredients; spread between slices of bread. Place bread on 28 × 18-inch piece of heavy-duty aluminum foil; wrap securely. Cover and grill bread 5 to 6 inches from medium coals, turning once, until cheese is melted, 8 to 10 minutes. Unwrap foil; grill bread uncovered 5 minutes longer. **24 slices**

PER SERVING: Calories 85; Protein 3 g; Carbohydrate 11 g; Fat 3 g; Cholesterol 5 mg; Sodium 180 mg

Sesame Bread

Cracker-like bread with sesame flavor, baked right on the grill for striped effect. Good with ribs or chicken.

2 cups Bisquick® original baking mix
¼ cup sesame seed
½ teaspoon salt
½ cup cold water
Margarine or butter (if desired)

Stir baking mix, sesame seed, salt and water to a soft dough. Gently smooth dough into a ball on floured surface. Knead 5 times.

Divide dough into halves. Roll or pat each half into a rectangle, 12 × 8 inches; cut lengthwise into halves.

Grill flat bread 5 inches from medium coals, turning once, 6 to 8 minutes. Cut each strip into 4 pieces. **16 pieces**

PER SERVING: Calories 65; Protein 1 g; Carbohydrate 9 g; Fat 3 g; Cholesterol 0 mg; Sodium 280 mg

Bruschetta on the Grill

Bruschetta is an Italian treat. Toasted—or grilled—bread is topped with garlic and olive oil. We've added fresh basil for a taste of summer.

1/2 cup olive oil
2 tablespoons chopped fresh or 2 teaspoons dried basil leaves
2 cloves garlic, crushed
1 loaf French bread (about 12 inches)

Mix oil, basil and garlic in small bowl. Cut bread lengthwise into 2 pieces. Brush with oil mixture. Grill over medium coals 6 minutes, turning once, until golden brown. Cut into 1/2-inch slices.

10 servings

PER SERVING: Calories 175; Protein 4 g; Carbohydrate 26 g; Fat 6 g; Cholesterol 0 mg; Sodium 270 mg

Grilled Lime Tortillas

If there isn't room on your grill for 2 large tortillas, cut each tortilla into 6 or 8 wedges before grilling.

2 tablespoons margarine or butter
1/2 teaspoon grated lime peel
2 teaspoons lime juice
2 ten-inch flour tortillas

Heat margarine until melted. Stir in lime peel and lime juice. Brush on both sides of tortillas.

Grill tortillas 5 to 6 inches from medium coals 5 to 6 minutes, turning once, until golden brown. Sprinkle with salt if desired. Cool slightly. Break into pieces.

2 servings

PER SERVING: Calories 185; Protein 2 g; Carbohydrate 19 g; Fat 12 g; Cholesterol 0 mg; Sodium 180 mg

Grilled Garlic with French Bread

If you like, you can use an herb-flavored olive oil in this unusual side dish.

2 large garlic bulbs
2 tablespoons olive or vegetable oil
12 thin slices French bread

Peel loose paperlike layers from garlic bulbs, but do not separate cloves. Place each garlic bulb on 12-inch square of heavy-duty aluminum foil. Brush generously with oil. Wrap bulbs securely in foil. Cover and grill 4 inches from medium coals 25 to 35 minutes or until garlic cloves are very soft.

Grill bread 4 inches from medium coals about 5 minutes, turning once, until golden brown. To serve, squeeze garlic out of individual cloves onto bread.

6 servings

PER SERVING: Calories 120; Protein 3 g; Carbohydrate 19 g; Fat 3 g; Cholesterol 0 mg; Sodium 180 mg

Quick Cleanup

Grilling cleanup is easy with these simple tips:

- Before grilling, brush the cooking surface with vegetable oil to prevent sticking.
- After grilling, scrape the cooking surface with a stiff wire brush.
- To keep the firebox of your charcoal grill clean, line it with heavy-duty aluminum foil. When the ashes have cooled, lift out the foil and slide ashes into the trash. The foil can be reused several times.
- Clean gas or electric grill cooking surfaces by closing the lid and turning the burners on high for about 15 minutes.

Bread in Foil

Quick and easy seasoned bread to round out a meal.

Cut 1 loaf (1 pound) French bread into 1-inch slices or Vienna bread into ½-inch slices, cutting almost to bottom of loaf. Spread one of the following Butter Spreads between slices of bread. Wrap in 28 × 18-inch piece of heavy-duty aluminum foil and seal securely. Grill bread 4 inches from medium coals, turning once, until hot, 15 to 20 minutes. **24 to 28 slices**

PER SERVING: Calories 90; Protein 2 g; Carbohydrate 11 g; Fat 4 g; Cholesterol 0 mg; Sodium 160 mg

Garlic Butter Spread

½ cup (1 stick) margarine or butter, softened
1 medium clove garlic, crushed

Mix ingredients.

Herb-Cheese Butter Spread

½ cup (1 stick) margarine or butter, softened
2 teaspoons chopped fresh parsley
½ teaspoon dried oregano leaves
2 tablespoons grated Parmesan cheese
⅛ teaspoon garlic salt

Mix all ingredients.

Herb-Lemon Butter Spread

½ cup (1 stick) margarine or butter, softened
2 teaspoons lemon juice
1 tablespoon chopped fresh herbs or 1 teaspoon dried herbs
Dash of salt

Mix all ingredients.

Pineapple–Angel Food Dessert

If you like, serve this warm, fruity dessert with vanilla ice cream.

1 can (8 ounce) crushed pineapple, drained
¼ cup orange marmalade
4 slices angel food cake, 1½ inches thick

Mix the pineapple and marmalade in small pan on grill. Grill about 6 inches from medium coals 6 to 8 minutes, stirring occasionally, until warm.

Grill cake about 2 minutes, turning once, until golden brown. Top with warm pineapple mixture. **4 servings**

PER SERVING: Calories 220; Protein 3 g; Carbohydrate 53 g; Fat 0 g; Cholesterol 0 mg; Sodium 80 mg

Pound Cake S'mores

4 slices pound cake, 1 inch thick
20 miniature marshmallows (about ¼ cup)
20 semisweet chocolate chips (about 1 tablespoon)

Make horizontal cut in side of each slice of cake, forming a pocket. Fill each pocket with 5 marshmallows and 5 chocolate chips.

Cover and grill cake 5 to 6 inches from medium coals 2 to 3 minutes, turning once, until golden brown. **4 s'mores**

PER SERVING: Calories 145; Protein 2 g; Carbohydrate 20 g; Fat 6 g; Cholesterol 45 mg; Sodium 55 mg

Pineapple–Angel Food Dessert

Zucchini-Nut Cake

Cake for dessert without having to heat up the oven!

1/3 cup sliced almonds
1 cup Bisquick original baking mix
1/3 cup sugar
1/2 teaspoon ground cinnamon
1/2 cup shredded zucchini
2 tablespoons milk
1 egg
Almond Glaze (below)

Grease 8 3/4-inch foil pie pan; coat bottom and side with almonds. Beat remaining ingredients, except Almond Glaze, 3 strokes.

Pour into pan. Cover with greased sheet of heavy-duty aluminum foil; secure foil to pan with spring-type wooden clothespins. Grill cake over medium coals until edges are set, about 10 minutes. Invert pan; grill until cake springs back when touched lightly, about 5 minutes longer. Remove foil and cool slightly; invert onto serving plate. Drizzle Almond Glaze over cake.

6 servings

PER SERVING: Calories 220; Protein 4 g; Carbohydrate 35 g; Fat 9 g; Cholesterol 35 mg; Sodium 300 mg

Almond Glaze

1/2 cup powdered sugar
1/4 teaspoon almond extract
2 to 3 teaspoons milk

Mix all ingredients until smooth.

Apples Alfresco

Grill as many apples as you'd like to serve—one or more!

1 baking apple
1 tablespoon packed brown sugar
2 teaspoons red cinnamon candies
2 teaspoons lemon juice
1 pineapple spear
2 tablespoons Cinnamon Whipped Cream (below)

Wash apple; core to within 1/2 inch of bottom. Score skin 1/8 inch deep in petal design. Fill cavity with remaining ingredients except Cinnamon Whipped Cream. Wrap securely in a double layer of 8-inch square heavy-duty aluminum foil. Grill 4 inches from medium coals, 30 to 40 minutes or until soft. Serve with Cinnamon Whipped Cream.

1 serving

PER SERVING: Calories 265; Protein 1 g; Carbohydrate 54 g; Fat 5 g; Cholesterol 15 mg; Sodium 15 mg

Cinnamon Whipped Cream

1/2 cup whipping cream
1 tablespoon granulated sugar
1/2 teaspoon ground cinnamon

Beat all ingredients until stiff.

Peaches and Berries

4 peaches
½ cup blueberries
8 teaspoons packed brown sugar
4 teaspoons lemon juice

Wash and halve peaches; remove pits. Place each peach half on square of double thickness heavy-duty aluminum foil. Fill cavity with blueberries; sprinkle with about 2 teaspoons brown sugar and squeeze lemon on peach halves. Wrap securely in foil. Grill 3 inches from hot coals 18 to 20 minutes or on medium coals 10 to 15 minutes, turning once. **4 servings**

PER SERVING: Calories 90; Protein 1 g; Carbohydrate 21 g; Fat 0 g; Cholesterol 0 mg; Sodium 5 mg

Golden Pears

2 firm ripe unpeeled pears
¼ cup golden raisins
¼ cup shredded or flaked coconut
2 tablespoons orange marmalade

Fold four 18 × 12-inch pieces heavy-duty aluminum foil crosswise in half. Cut pears lengthwise into halves; remove cores. Place each half, cut side up, in center of piece of foil. Mix raisins, coconut and marmalade. Spoon about 2 tablespoons onto each pear half. Loosely wrap with foil. (Do not press foil down onto tops of pears.)

Grill foil packets 5 to 6 inches from medium coals 15 to 18 minutes or until pears are tender. **4 servings**

PER SERVING: Calories 125; Protein 1 g; Carbohydrate 29 g; Fat 2 g; Cholesterol 0 mg; Sodium 15 mg

Grilled Banana Boats

The amounts of peanut butter and chocolate chips you'll need will vary with the size of the bananas and your taste!

4 firm bananas
¼ cup peanut butter
1 tablespoon chocolate chips

Cut wedge in inside curve of unpeeled banana about ½-inch wide by ½ inch deep. (Cut through banana peel but leave it attached at one end.) Discard wedge of banana. Fill banana with peanut butter; dot with chocolate chips. Lay strip of banana peel back over chocolate chips.

Grill bananas, wedge sides up, 5 to 6 inches from medium coals 8 to 10 minutes or until peels are black and bananas begin to soften. Remove strip of peel. Eat with spoon. **4 bananas**

PER SERVING: Calories 220; Protein 5 g; Carbohydrate 33 g; Fat 9 g; Cholesterol 0 mg; Sodium 80 mg

Grilled Shortcake

2⅓ cups Bisquick original baking mix
3 tablespoons sugar
3 tablespoons margarine or butter, melted
½ cup milk
Fresh berries or mixed fruit
Sweetened whipped cream

Stir baking mix, sugar, margarine and milk to a soft dough. Spread dough in one greased 9-inch foil pie pan. Invert another greased 9-inch foil pie pan over pan with dough. Secure rims together with spring-type wooden clothespins. Grill shortcake 4 inches from hot coals, 15 minutes on each side or until brown. Serve warm with berries and whipped cream. **6 servings**

PER SERVING: Calories 310; Protein 4 g; Carbohydrate 42 g; Fat 14 g; Cholesterol 0 mg; Sodium 740 mg

METRIC CONVERSION GUIDE

U.S. UNITS	CANADIAN METRIC	AUSTRALIAN METRIC
Volume		
1/4 teaspoon	1 mL	1 ml
1/2 teaspoon	2 mL	2 ml
1 teaspoon	5 mL	5 ml
1 tablespoon	15 mL	20 ml
1/4 cup	50 mL	60 ml
1/3 cup	75 mL	80 ml
1/2 cup	125 mL	125 ml
2/3 cup	150 mL	170 ml
3/4 cup	175 mL	190 ml
1 cup	250 mL	250 ml
1 quart	1 liter	1 liter
1 1/2 quarts	1.5 liter	1.5 liter
2 quarts	2 liters	2 liters
2 1/2 quarts	2.5 liters	2.5 liters
3 quarts	3 liters	3 liters
4 quarts	4 liters	4 liters
Weight		
1 ounce	30 grams	30 grams
2 ounces	55 grams	60 grams
3 ounces	85 grams	90 grams
4 ounces (1/4 pound)	115 grams	125 grams
8 ounces (1/2 pound)	225 grams	225 grams
16 ounces (1 pound)	455 grams	500 grams
1 pound	455 grams	1/2 kilogram

Measurements

Inches	Centimeters
1	2.5
2	5.0
3	7.5
4	10.0
5	12.5
6	15.0
7	17.5
8	20.5
9	23.0
10	25.5
11	28.0
12	30.5
13	33.0
14	35.5
15	38.0

Temperatures

Fahrenheit	Celsius
32°	0°
212°	100°
250°	120°
275°	140°
300°	150°
325°	160°
350°	180°
375°	190°
400°	200°
425°	220°
450°	230°
475°	240°
500°	260°

NOTE
The recipes in this cookbook have not been developed or tested using metric measures. When converting recipes to metric, some variations in quality may be noted.

Index